THE DIETARY LAWS OF THE BIBLE

by Vic Lockman

To my wife Jean,
who is always telling me
what to eat
and
what not to eat.

Copyright © at Common Law, 1997 by Vic Lockman
ISBN 0-936175-31-1

Scripture quotations are from the
MODERN KING JAMES VERSION
OF THE BIBLE
Published by Sovereign Grace Publishers
Lafayette, Indiana

Published by
Vic Lockman
P.O. Box 1396
Yreka, Ca. 96097

TABLE OF CONTENTS

Introduction 1
Preface 5

PART I - THE DIETARY LAWS OF THE BIBLE

1. Leviticus XI 11
2. A "DIGEST" of Leviticus XI 17

PART II - TO EAT OR NOT TO EAT

3. Peter's Vision 25
4. The New Testament "Flavor" 33
5. The Common, the Unclean, and the Abominable 37
6. The Rest of the Story 41
7. "OH, YUCK!" 51

PART III - THE CREATION KEY

8. The Creation Key 63
9. Is There More to the Story 71

PART IV - THE NEW CREATION

10. The New Heavens and the New Earth 85
11. God's Diet for Modern Man,
    Ten Commandments for a Healthy Body 89

APPENDIX

Food Images in Dreams and Visions 95
Transfer Theology 97
John Calvin and the Dietary Laws 98
Third World Conditions Foster Tapeworm Cysts 100
Will the Real Bible Please Stand Up? 102

INTRODUCTION

The Bible clearly places salvation beyond attainment by any manner of works-righteousness or law-keeping: "For by grace are you saved through faith, and that not of yourselves, it is the gift of God, not of works, lest any man should boast" (Ep.2:8-9). Yet in the same breath we are told that: "we are his workmanship, created in Christ Jesus unto good works, which God has before ordained that we should walk in them"(Ep.2:10).

Both salvation and good works are possible only because of the work of God the Holy Spirit within us: He regenerates our spiritually dead souls (Titus 3:5,6) and causes us to walk in His statutes (Ezek.36:25-27)-"It is God who works in you both to will and to do of His good pleasure"(Phil.2:13).

Jesus made it clear that if we love Him we will keep His commandments (Jn.14:15), and His commandments are not burdensome (I Jn.5:3), and that this is of extended temporal duration: "Do not think that I have come to destroy the law or the prophets. I came not to destroy but to fulfill. For truly I say to you, Till heaven and earth pass away, not one jot or tittle shall in any way pass from the law until all is fulfilled. Therefore, whoever shall break one of these commandments, the least, and shall teach men so, he shall be called the least in the kingdom of Heaven, and whosoever shall do and teach them, the same shall be called great in the kingdom of heaven" (Mt.5:17-19).

This means that every single law of the Older Covenant continues to be valid and is intended to be obeyed by the New Covenant church unless it is directly abrogated in the scriptures of the New Testament, implied by apostolic example, or by valid inference made obsolete. The book of Hebrews, in its many references to the Older Covenant form of worship, indicates that the former system composed of shadows and types of heavenly things, has been superseded by Christ the very object of that imagery, for He is "the Mediator of a better covenant"(Heb.8:6). The imagery, the ceremonies, the priesthood, and the temple itself all pointed ahead to the divine High Priest, the Lord Jesus Christ. Hebrews 8:5, quoting Ex.25:40: "See that you make all things according to the pattern shown you in the mountain," tells us that those priests of old and the system in which they labored, which included the pattern of the tabernacle, served "as example and shadow of heavenly things." The writer goes on at length in this vein: "Now that which decays and becomes old is ready to vanish away"(8:13); the old tabernacle was until the time of reformation (9:1-10); these were expendable patterns of heavenly things (9:23); and the ceremonial law was a shadow of good things to come (10:1). Jesus Christ was the realization of all these images, having fulfilled them in His sinless life on earth, substitutionary blood atonement, bodily resurrection and ascension, and messianic reign over all creation from Heaven until the last day (He.10:10-13). Today the ceremonial laws of Israel are "out of gear," no longer observed on earth by man, but eternally exercised in heaven (He.7:25). In this way, and in this way alone, they have abiding validity (Mt.5:18).

"Out of gear" also are those laws of various particulars of Israel's life as God's covenant people, laws of territorial inheritance (Nu.34), now broadened for the New Israel of God to include the whole earth (Mt.5:5); the sign of covenant admission, circumcision, being replaced by baptism (Col.2:11 -12), and covenantal-life-maintenance, the Passover (Ex.12:1ff), being replaced by the Lord's Supper (Lu.22:14-20; I Cor.5:7); and the special holy days and ceremonial sabbaths, being fulfilled by Christ and coalesced into ONE holy day, the Lord's Day, which is the first day of the week (Jn.20:19) and patterned on the creation sabbath or day of rest (Gen.2:1-3), now a time-monument to Christ's having established the new creation day of eternal rest for all those who rest in Him from their labors (He.4:9,10).

The Older Covenant gave way to the new at the cross in principle, and, as a practical matter, in 70 A.D. at the fall of Jerusalem which signaled an historic culmination of the Jewish kingdom with the destruction of the temple. And thus, there is a great divide of the old from the new.

It is the view of this book, contrary to popular belief and general ignorance, that while any ceremonial aspect there may have been to the dietary laws of the Old Testament has ceased with the demise of the nation Israel, those laws are still valid today for all men in all nations (and particularly for Christians), being an inseparable part of God's creation-law-order. These dietary laws constitute God's prescribed health-menu, and in the keeping of them is great reward; good health and longevity, all of which are effective in a more strenuous proclamation of the Gospel and its resulting worldwide planting of His righteous kingdom.

Give it a hearing, and see if you won't agree that there stands a very formidable prima-facie case for the continuing validity and observation of the dietary laws today.

Here's to your health!

Vic Lockman, Yreka, Ca. 1997

PREFACE

This book has roots reaching back many years in my Christian life, to the time when I came under the teaching of R. J. Rushdoony for a period of four years as he was giving a series of lectures which were later to become published as THE INSTITUTES OF BIBLICAL LAW, VOLUME I (1973). His itemization of the health and dietary laws of the Old Testament, along with explanations of why certain things are or are not unhealthy was extremely enlightening. His simple and sound interpretation of Peter's vision in Acts X made it all too apparent that most Christians were badly mistaken in believing that the dietary laws were abrogated along with the ceremonial laws of Israel at the advent of the New Covenant era. Rushdoony's outline of the health laws organizes those precepts very logically, and below I have abbreviated his outline and combined some of its points.

1. The eating of blood is forbidden; the animal cannot be strangled; it must be bled (Lev. 17:10-14; 19:26; Ac. 15:20). Consumption of animal fats are also forbidden (Lev. 7:23,25).

2. Dead, unbutchered animals are forbidden fare (animals that die on their own- Deut. 14:21). Also forbidden is the flesh of any animal torn by wild beasts (Ex.22:31).

3. Most scavenger quadrupeds, birds, fish, and insects are prohibited, as well as scavenger organs which clear the body of impurities (Lev.3:9-11).

4. Carnivorous animals are forbidden food.

5. Herbivorous animals are allowed, unless they neither chew the cud nor divide the hoof (the horse). Also allowed are grain feeding birds.

6. Most insects, with the exception of certain (multistomached) locusts or grasshoppers are forbidden (Lev. 11:22; Mt. 3:4).

7. No legislation is given respecting fruits, grains, eggs, and vegetables; hence they are fit for human consumption, unless, in the case of animal products (eggs, milk, cheese), they are derived from unclean beasts. Mushrooms (fungi) are forbidden because they are not seed-bearing plants (Gen.1:29).

8. The terms of division are clean, common, and unclean, the latter flesh condemned as an abomination.

9. All foods and liquids left in uncovered vessels in the vicinity of a dying or dead person are forbidden (Nu. 19:14,15).

10. It is forbidden to boil a kid in its mother's milk (Ex. 23:19; 34:26; De.14:21).

11. Wine, in moderation, may be part of the diet (I Tim. 5:23).

12. Human waste is to be buried outside the camp (Deut. 23:12,13).

13. Quarantine (a means of isolating disease) is required (Nu. 5:2-4).

God so loved the natural world that he created it with its very own sanitation crew, the unclean animals, many of which dispose of dead carcasses, dung, and other impurities. God loved mankind in that he gave us scientifically sound laws of sanitation, hygiene, and diet far in advance of man's own developing disciplines along these lines. Thousands of years before Pasteur, God instructed Israel in the ways of sanitation and health, so that even in the days of relatively primitive knowledge and medicine, these laws would go far along the path of preventive medicine and longevity. Yet, even in our own day, there are still cultures that disobey God's simple laws of health, to their own harm.

Secondly, I am indebted to the Rev. Elmer A. Josephson, whose book GOD'S KEY TO HEALTH AND HAPPINESS (1962), came into my hands shortly after my Rushdoony encounter. Mr. Josephson stated the whole concept in a very serious and loving way, and answered the questions of the critics. This was all encompassed in an evangelical approach.

I am also grateful to numerous other Christians, whose views, both pro and con on this subject, have had an influence on my thinking and apologetic method.

Recognizing that all things were made by, through, and for our Lord and Savior Jesus Christ, I credit Him, in whom reside all the treasures of wisdom and knowledge, for what measure of truth is contained in this little book. I pray God's blessings on the contents of this book so far as they accurately reflect His will for our lives.

Go ahead now, imitate the faithful Bereans to see if these things are so.

-VIC LOCKMAN

PART I

THE DIETARY LAWS OF THE BIBLE

1
GOD'S DIETARY LAWS

Leviticus was the first book that Jewish children used to study in the Synagogue. Today it is more likely to occupy last place, or none at all, in the church's preference for reading or study. Regulations for sacrifice and uncleanness hold little interest for modern man. It is therefore not surprising that few moderns know anything of the dietary laws of Leviticus XI and Deuteronomy XIV. Hopefully, what follows in this book will revive a healthy interest in those ancient, but still very necessary laws of God.

LEVITICUS XI

1 And the LORD spoke to Moses and to Aaron, saying to them,
2 Speak to the sons of Israel, saying, These are the animals which you shall eat among all the animals that are in the earth.
3 Whatever divides the hoof, and is cloven-footed, chewing the cud, among the animals, that you shall eat.
4 Only, you shall not eat these of them that chew the cud, or of them that divide the hoof: the camel, for he

chews the cud but does not divide the hoof; he is unclean to you.
5 And the coney, because he chews the cud but does not divide the hoof; he is unclean to you.
6 And the hare, because he chews the cud but does not divide the hoof; he is unclean to you.
7 And the swine, though he divides the hoof and is cloven-footed, yet he does not chew the cud; he is unclean to you.
8 You shall not eat of their flesh, and you shall not touch their dead body. They are unclean to you.
9 These you shall eat of all that are in the waters: whatever has fins and scales in the waters, in the seas, and in the rivers, them you shall eat.
10 And all that have not fins and scales in the seas, and in the rivers, and all that move in the waters, and of any living thing that is in the waters, they shall be an abomination to you.
11 They shall even be an abomination to you. You shall not eat of their flesh, but you shall have their carcasses in abomination.
12 Whatever has no fins nor scales in the waters shall be an abomination to you.
13 And you shall have these in abomination among the fowls. They shall not be eaten, they are an abomination: the eagle, and the black vulture, and the bearded vulture,
14 and the kite, and the falcon, according to its kind;
15 every raven according to its kind;
16 and the ostrich, and the great owl, and the gull,

and small hawks,
17 and the little owl, and the cormorant, and the eared owl;
18 and the barn owl, and the pelican, and the owl-vulture;
19 and the stork, the heron according to its kind, and the hoopoe, and the bat.
20 Every flying swarming creature going on all four, it is an abomination to you.
21 Yet you may eat these of any flying swarming thing that goes on all four, those which have legs above their feet, to leap with on the earth.
22 You may eat these of them: the locust after its kind, and the bald locust after its kind, and the long horned locust after its kind, and the short horned grasshopper after its kind.
23 But every other flying swarming thing which has four feet shall be an abomination to you.
24 And you shall be unclean for these. Whoever touches their dead body shall be unclean until evening.
25 And whoever carries the carcass of them shall wash his clothes and be unclean until the evening;
26 even every living thing which divides the hoof, and is not cloven- footed, nor chews the cud, they are unclean to you. Everyone that touches them shall be unclean.
27 And whatever goes on its paws, among all the living things that go on all four, those are unclean to you. Whoever touches their dead body shall be unclean until the evening.

28 And he that carries their dead bodies shall wash his clothes and be unclean until the evening. They are unclean to you.
29 These also shall be unclean to you among the swarming things that swarm on the earth: the weasel, and the mouse, and the great lizard after its kind; 30 and the gecko, and the monitor, and the lizard, and the sand lizard, and the brown owl.
31 These are unclean to you among all that swarm. Whoever touches them when they are dead shall be unclean until the evening.
32 And whatever shall fall on any of them when they are dead, shall be unclean, whether any vessel of wood, or clothing, or skin, or sack; whatever vessel in which work is done, it must be put into water, and it shall be unclean to the evening. So it shall be cleaned.
33 And any earthen vessel in which any of them falls, whatever is in it shall be unclean. And you shall break it.
34 Of all food which may be eaten, that on which such water comes shall be unclean. And all drink that may be drunk in every such vessel shall be unclean.
35 And every thing on which any part of their dead body falls shall be unclean; whether it is the oven, or ranges for pots, they shall be broken down. They are unclean and shall be unclean to you.
36 But a fountain or pit, in which there is a collection of water, shall be clean. But that which touches their dead body shall be unclean.
37 And if any of their dead body falls on any sowing

seed which is to be sown, it shall be unclean.
38 But if any water is put on the seed, and any part of the dead body falls on it, it shall be unclean to you.
39 And if any animal among those you may eat dies, he that touches its dead body shall be unclean until the evening.
40 And he that eats of its dead body shall wash his clothes and be unclean until the evening. He also that carries its body shall wash his clothes and be unclean until the evening.
41 And every swarming thing that swarms on the earth shall be an abomination. It shall not be eaten.
42 Anything going on its belly, and any going on all four, and all having many feet, even every swarming thing that swarms on the earth, you shall not eat them. For they are an abomination.
43 You shall not defile yourselves with any swarming thing that swarms, neither shall you make yourselves unclean with them, so that you should be defiled by them.
44 For I am the LORD your God, and you shall sanctify yourselves, and you shall be holy, for I am holy. Neither shall you defile yourselves with any kind of swarming thing that swarms on the earth.
45 For I am the LORD who brings you up out of the land of Egypt, to be your God. You shall therefore be holy, for I am holy.
46 This is the law of the animals, and of the fowl, and of every living creature that moves in the waters, and of every creature that swarms on the earth,

47 to make a difference between the unclean and the clean, and between the beast that may be eaten and the beast that may not be eaten.

2
A "DIGEST" OF LEVITICUS XI

"The LORD spoke to Moses and to Aaron"(vs.1), that is, He spoke to both the CIVIL and the ECCLESIASTICAL rulers in Israel. Here is an initial indication of the wholeness of life involved.

Jamieson, Fausset, & Brown, in their commentary, say that, "These laws, therefore, being subservient to sanitary as well as religious ends, were addressed to both Moses and Aaron." These commentators further discuss the unhealthy and diseased condition of many unclean animals, citing Whitlaw's Code of Health (pg.9). They note that animals which both chew the cud and part the hoof have been favored in most countries, though observed most carefully by the people who were favored with the promulgation of God's law. They identify the swine as a filthy, foul-feeding animal.

The dietary laws, standing first in the general precepts of clean and unclean, are, in accordance with the Hebrew division of the animal kingdom, listed under four main headings: (1) the quadrupeds, or land animals, (2) the water animals, (3) the birds of the air, and (4) the swarming things. These are pretty much classifications based on the habitat and general activity of the creatures. For instance, bats are found listed among birds. Modern classifications are, of course, of different divisions and are further broken down into class, order, family, genus, and species, and these contain subdivisions as well.

The important division that cuts through all classes is that of clean and unclean. These distinctions, based on the physical and dining habits as well as the digestive systems of the animals, may be summarized as follows.

LAND ANIMALS: those that chew the cud (having a complex digestive system) and completely divide the hoof or foot (beneath as well as above) are clean. Those that have a simple digestive system and do not completely divide the hoof or foot, such as horses, are unclean.

WATER ANIMALS: those having both fins and scales are clean. It is overlapping scales that qualify and not separated or spiny plates or ridges that leave the skin exposed. All else are declared unclean.

BIRDS OF THE AIR: those not prohibited are the grain eating birds, and those listed as forbidden are carnivorous birds of prey and scavengers.

SWARMING THINGS: this is a large collection of various creatures, such as insects, small rodents, reptiles, etc., and they are identified by name rather than physical characteristics. Swarmers are to be found on land, in the sea, and in the air. Mostly these are unclean. A surprising exception is four kinds of locust or grasshopper (vs.21-23), which incidentally, have a complex digestive system.

In general, it may be said that the unclean animals are those which are in direct contact with their environment and the parasites therein (paws, no scales, etc.), possessing a simple digestive system that works rapidly and does not break down the food very well, and those creatures which are scavengers or beasts of prey.

The book of Leviticus continues to discuss uncleanness in other areas of life; childbirth (Chapter 12), diseases (chapter 13), and body-discharges, none of which are subjects of this study. They are all in the context of ceremonial uncleanness as a barrier to communion with God, but like the dietary laws, they have their roots in the real world of pollution. Keil and Delitzch's Old Testament Commentary ruminates further along these lines, saying, "Ceremonially, all of these things reminded men that in all the processes of life—generation, birth, eating, disease, and death—how everything, even his own bodily nature, lies under the curse of sin (Gen. 3:14-19), so that the law might serve as a schoolmaster to bring men to Christ."

While denying the undergirding of the dietary laws for any sanitary reasons, Keil and Delitzch nonetheless cannot help but discern their real-world connection: "...the Mosaic law followed the marks laid down by tradition, which took its rise in the primeval age, whose childlike mind, acute perception, and deep intuitive insight into nature generally, discerned more truly and essentially the real nature of the animal creation than we shall ever be able to do, with thoughts and perceptions disturbed as ours are by the influences of unnatural and ungodly culture." And then in another place: "Hence in all the nations and in all the religions of antiquity we find that contrast between clean and unclean, which was developed in a dualistic form, it is true, in many of the religious systems, but had its primary root in the corruption that had entered the world through sin."

Keil also observes that: "All animals are unclean which bear the image of sin, of death and corruption...of winged creatures not only birds of prey...but also marsh birds and others, which live on worms, carrion, and all sorts of impurities" (Keil, Biblical Archeology II, pp.118ff).

Even the world's greatest biblical scholars, while denying that any sanitation or health reasons are the basis for the dietary laws, cannot help but expose their own gut-feelings about the unclean creatures in such verbiage as quoted above. Man cannot, in a sense, help but bear witness to the stark realities of the world about him. He argues against himself at points, as we have seen, because God speaks so loudly through natural revelation at times that He drowns out the wisdom of man's intellect.

Finally, we need to recognize and take to heart the wholeness that underlies God's creation, as the very word "universe" indicates. There are three spheres in the world; atmosphere, land, and sea, and each is populated with both clean and unclean creatures, all of whom are expected to obey the law of God in its normative provisions, but with certain lower-creature circumscriptions, of course. Both man and his beast must keep the Sabbath, for example (Ex.20:10). The ox that gores a man must be put to death (Ex. 21:28). Killer-animals, by drawing blood, are also doomed to having their own blood drawn by beasts stronger than themselves. The death penalty among beasts! Those that eat blood have their blood eaten. Those that eat putrefying flesh, rife with parasites and plagues, may also expect to be devoured by those same internally infernal ugly-wigglies.

As for man, God demands total commitment, this being the essence of covenantal faith. No dark corner of man's life lies outside the pale of the covenant...it is a covenant of holy wholeness!

"Therefore you shall KEEP ALL THE COMMANDMENTS which I command you today, so that you may be strong and go in and possess the land where you go to possess it, and so that you may MAKE YOUR DAYS LONGER in the land which the LORD swore to your fathers to give to them and to their seed a land that flows with milk and honey" (emphasis added).
Deuteronomy 11:8,9

PART 2

TO EAT OR NOT TO EAT

3
PETER'S VISION

THE ACTS OF THE APOSTLES
Chapter X

1 And a certain man named Cornelius was in Caesarea, a centurion of the Italian cohort,
2 one devout and fearing God, with all his household, both doing many alms to the people, and praying continually to God.
3 About the ninth hour of the day he saw plainly in a vision an angel of God coming to him and saying to him, Cornelius!
4 And he was gazing at him, and becoming terrified, he said, What is it, lord? And he said to him, Your prayers and your alms have come up for a memorial before God.
5 And now send men to Joppa and call for Simeon, whose last name is Peter.
6 He is staying with one Simon a tanner, whose house is by the seaside. He will tell you what you must do.
7 And when the angel who spoke to Cornelius departed, he called two of his servants, and a devout soldier from those who waited on him continually.
8 And explaining all things to them, he sent them to

Joppa.

9 On the next day, as these went on the road, and drawing near to the city, Peter went up on the housetop to pray, about the sixth hour.

10 And he became very hungry and desired to eat. But while they made ready, an ecstasy fell on him.

11 And he saw the heaven opened and a certain vessel like a sheet coming down to him, being bound at the four corners and let down to the earth;

12 in which were all the four-footed animals of the earth, and the wild beasts, and the reptiles, and the birds of heaven.

13 And a voice came to him, saying, Rise, Peter! Kill and eat!

14 But Peter said, not so, Lord, for I have never eaten anything that is common or unclean.

15 And the voice spoke to him again the second time, What God has made clean, you do not call common.

16 This happened three times, and the vessel was received up again into the heaven.

17 And while Peter doubted within himself what the vision which he had seen might be, behold, the men who were sent from Cornelius had asked for Simon's house and stood on the porch.

18 And they called and asked if Simon whose last name is Peter was staying there.

19 And while Peter thought on the vision, the Spirit said to him, Behold, three men are looking for you.

20 Therefore arise and go down and go with them without doubting, for I have sent them.

21 And going down to the men, those sent to him from Cornelius, Peter said, Behold, I am the one you are seeking. For what reason have you come?
22 And they said, Cornelius the centurion, a just man and one who fears God, and one of good report among all the nation of the Jews, was warned from God by a holy angel to send for you to come to his house and to hear words from you.
23 Then he called them in and lodged them. And on the next day Peter went away with them, and certain brothers from Joppa went with him.
24 And the next day they entered into Caesarea. And Cornelius was waiting for them, and had called together his kinsmen and near friends.
25 And as Peter was coming in, Cornelius met him and fell down at his feet and worshiped.
26 But Peter took him up, saying, Stand up! I also am a man myself.
27 And as he talked with him, he went in and found many who had come together.
28 And he said to them, You know that it is an unlawful thing for a man who is a Jew to keep company with or come near to one of another nation. But God has shown me that I should not call any man common or unclean.

   Ordinarily, in a more sensible hermeneutical-environment, this discussion would begin at the beginning, at the creation account in Genesis one. But for the sake of being where the practical-theology tire hits the barren road of gut-doctrine, i.e., "if it tastes good I'll eat it!," this argument opens at Acts ten, the rhetorical playground of the swine-diners throughout Christendom.

Peter had a vision of a great sheet full of unclean animals being let down from heaven and lifted up again three times, accompanied by a voice saying, "Rise, Peter. Kill and eat"(Acts 10:13). Although Peter was puzzled as to the meaning of this, advocates of the eat-anything-that-moves school believe that this vision or ecstasy repeals the biblical dietary laws, slam-dunk; and they hasten to seize a hog and carve off a juicy slice! And with this presupposition, the whole New Testament doctrine of diet is interpreted.

Such is hailed as a bountiful blessing and a great victory for dietary freedom. Now Israelites and Gentiles alike can wallow taste bud deep, not only in swine, but hordes of parasites, bacteria, and virus ridden denizens of the grimy-deep to the fowl-filled skies above. Not to mention all the yummy blood, maggots, slugs and every wiggly larvae on the manure heap. Ah-h, delicious dietary liberty! Admitting that the vision addresses bringing the gospel to the nations hardly quenches their salivation for unclean meat.

Now let's give Peter's vision more scrupulous scrutiny. Namely let's critique the passage context-wise, the immediate and later the Bible-wide context.

Acts ten is a two-act play of sorts. It contains, first of all, the vision of Cornelius, a Roman Centurion, stationed in Caesarea. "He saw plainly in a vision an angel of God"...who gave him a forthright command to send men to Peter in Joppa, instructing them to do whatever Peter says. Cornelius does exactly as bidden, without the slightest hesitation on his part. There is nothing obscure or symbolic about the vision. We could say that the vision was of a LITERAL nature! Similar direct, literal revelations of God to men are not uncommon in the Book of Acts. In chapter nine, Paul, blinded at his conversion, was told to "Arise and go into the city..."which he did. Meanwhile, in Damascus, Ananias received a vision in which he was told to meet Paul, restore his vision, and baptize him. Both visions were given as, and received as, direct literal revelations and commands from God. In chapter 16 Paul, by vision, was instructed to go to Macedonia. He went! In chapter twenty-three, the Lord stood by Paul and told him: "you also must bear witness at Rome" (vs.11). He did!

Nobody failed to comprehend or obey such direct divine marching orders. Balk, yes, as did Jonah (Jon.1:1-3), but "No comprende?" ...never! Twice God told Elijah to "Arise, eat," and he ate (I Kings 19:7,8).

So Cornelius first received his vision, and in obedience, sent three men to Joppa to find Peter. And the next day while Peter was praying on the rooftop of Simon the tanner, and becoming very hungry, he received a vision (or ecstasy) from God, tailored to fit his condition, and thereby guaranteed to gain his rapt attention.

The sheet full of unclean beasts, thrice lowered from heaven with the command to kill and eat must have been an awesome sight, quite out of the ordinary. It's the kind of experience one doesn't have in the normal course of life. In other words, it reeks of imagery, not literalism. That's how it impressed Peter, and he DOUBTED what it might mean. Is that possible with a literal vision? "Kill! Eat!"...the command form, the Greek imperative? The Lord's imperatives aren't taken lightly or without notice and understanding elsewhere in the Book of Acts, nor at any other place in the Bible.

"Peace, be still!" said Jesus to the raging sea, and immediately it was calm (Mk 4:39). Paul, referring to his conversion when the Lord appeared to him on the road to Damascus, said, "I did not disobey the heavenly vision" (Acts 26:19). "Take! Eat!" the Lord commanded at his last supper, and nary a man, not even Judas, declined or delayed (Mk 14:22). "Lazarus, come Forth!" cried Jesus outside the tomb, and even the dead didn't dilly-dally (Jn. 11:43)!

But what did Peter do in response to the divine imperative? Did he hurry down to the local Piggly Wiggly market and pig-out? Quite the contrary. He walked away pondering the meaning of the vision. In fact, throughout the Book of Acts there is evidence that the dietary laws were of continuing validity, and throughout the life of the Apostle Peter we find strong and undeniable indicators that his attitude toward the "unclean" diet was unchanged. "Unclean" continued to be a dirty word for Peter, as we shall shortly see.

What is apparent from the inspired record is that Peter had a truly biblically sound hermeneutical modus-operandi. He believed that scripture interprets scripture, i.e., GOD interprets his own word. In this regard Peter is much like Joseph in Egypt who also waited for God to interpret symbolic dreams involving food that meant something else. By Peter's inaction at the command to kill and to eat in the vision, he assented with Joseph that interpretations belong to God...NOT MEN (Genesis 40:8)! (See *Food Images in Dreams and Visions* in the Appendix.) And sure enough, immediately after the vision, Cornelius' three messengers arrived (note: three lowerings of the sheet = three gentile messengers) Soon thereafter Peter showed that he understood the imagery of his vision when he declared, "But God has shown me that I should not call any man common or unclean"(Acts 10:28)!

The nations are thereafter on an even footing with Israel, being grafted into the covenant (Rom.11:17).The vision has nothing to do with diet! It is a symbolic vision, not meant by its author to be taken literally.

G. Campbell Morgan, noted theologian who wrote over fifty Bible commentaries, has this to say about the nature of the visions in Acts ten: "The vision of Cornelius was objective, and needed no explanation, for the instructions given to the Gentile soldier were perfectly clear and definite. All that was necessary was that Cornelius should obey, and discover the issues of revelation. That of Peter, on the other hand, was subjective, and needed interpretation." He also says that, "So far as the commandments against certain forms of animal life were ceremonial, they are swept away; but so far as they were laws of health, they abide" (The Acts of the Apostles, G. Campbell Morgan, pg.270, 273).

We believe that they are ALL health laws and it was secondary that the "clean" animals were acceptable for sacrifice and the "unclean" forbidden.

Many Christians view the vision in reverse: they think that the Jewish converts to Christianity were thereafter dragged down to the same unsavory menu-level as the nations. Whereas the truth of the matter is that the nations henceforth, by invitation to the marriage supper of the lamb (inclusion in the covenant), were also literally ushered into a higher, healthier, and holier dining room, God's clean chow cafe!

"God is great, God is good, and we thank him for our food!"

4
THE NEW TESTAMENT FLAVOR

The flavor of the New Testament is predominantly a negative one in its references to unclean animals. They are commonly employed in comparisons of good and bad, and as synonyms for less than upright characters. Jesus cautions us not to give that which is holy to dogs, nor to cast our pearls before swine (Mt.7:6). He says, "or what man is there of you, if his son asks a loaf, will he give him a stone? Or if he asks a fish, will he give him a snake" (Mt. 7:9-10)? He called false prophets wolves in sheep's clothing (Mt. 7:15). He called Herod a fox (Lu.13:32), and the Scribes and Pharisees, "offspring of vipers" (Mt.12:34).

In Matthew 13:47-50, Christ's parable of the dragnet, picturing the separation of the just from the unjust on Judgment Day, the fishermen gathered the GOOD fish into vessels, but threw away the BAD. He used for "Good" the Greek word "katharos" (clean), and for the "BAD," "akatharos" (unclean). Clearly the "clean" fish are the good men or the saved, and the "unclean" are the unsaved. So we see here that the unclean even have a tie-in to damnation and hell-fire.

In Jesus encounter with a woman who had a demon-possessed daughter, both Jesus and the woman herself used the metaphor of "dogs" in their reference to Gentiles (Mark 7:24-30). Isaiah also identified the Gentiles as the "unclean ones" (Isa.52:1).

JESUS THE SWINE-KILLER

In His healing of the Gadarene demon infested maniac, the Lord did a rather amazing thing in sending the legion of demons into a herd of swine which, as a result, were destroyed by rushing into the sea (Mark 5:1-20). He initiated the total destruction of a valuable herd of two thousand pigs, the property of strangers who had done Him no harm. Is this a lesson on "doing unto others what they don't deserve?" Does this extremely destructive act exemplify the biblical teaching on loving your neighbor and looking out not only for your own interest but those of others? Is it consistent with the biblical teaching on personal responsibility and accountability for acts that diminish your neighbor's material well-being? Or can it be interpreted with pietistic rationale that says, "A human being is worth more than thousands of swine?" Or may we logically reason that the Savior's miracles are so precious that they can scarcely be measured in terms of earthly wealth?

It should be evident to the reader who recognizes and values the consistency of biblical ethics that none of the above explanations are satisfactory. The answer, and not an obscure one, lies elsewhere.

Actually, Christ's act in destroying the swine may be viewed from several perspectives, all issuing from the central truth that pigs have always been on God's no-no list for human consumption.

First, linguistically: three dimensions of the account center on the word "unclean" (akathartos), the inherently contaminated. Swine are unclean (Lev.11:7,8); demons are unclean (Lu.4:33); and Gentiles (the Gadarene community) are unclean (compared to "dogs" in Mark 7:25-30).

The exorcism, in this light, may be viewed as Gospel-judgment; both the disobedient Gentiles and the fruit of their err, the swine, are punished, and the demons themselves receive a down-payment on their ultimate destruction when they will be cast into a different kind of lake, an eternal lake of fire, at Judgment Day!

The exorcism also presented two prospective blessings, physical and spiritual. Certainly, many thousands of pounds of an unhealthy fare would never be consumed, and, had the Gadarenes taken the entire matter to heart, they would have reexamined the facts concerning such animals and their origin, i.e., the Creator's purpose for scavenger beasts. This would have been an immense boon to the health of the community.

Secondly, the massacre of the swine was an open door to repentance. Judgment, repentance, and restoration are a common scriptural pattern (II Chron. 7:14).

The sad response, however, was a hardening of hearts against the Savior. Truly, their god was their belly, quite literally (Phil. 3:19).

Of final note, it is significant that on no other occasion during His ministry, did the Lord Jesus Christ indulge in such a wanton destruction of private property; not in the name of a "good deed," nor for any other reason. True, the Temple cleansing, though rough stuff, did not result in any recorded destruction of property.

The commentator who fails to recognize the status of "unclean" spirits, swine, and Gentiles, is overlooking the heart of the message, perhaps doing so in blind deference to the traditional church teaching that you can eat anything that moves!

And last, but not least, the beloved Apostle John, in the last great book of the Bible, the Book of the Revelation of Jesus Christ, was inspired by the Lord to inscribe a grand-slam of uncleanness all in the one verse, the thirteenth of chapter sixteen: "And I saw three UNCLEAN SPIRITS like FROGS come out of the mouth of the DRAGON, and out of the mouth of the BEAST, and out of the mouth of the FALSE PROPHET!" (Emphasis added for obvious reasons). How much uncleanness can be packed into one sentence? It almost defies expository expertise...therefore, I'll close without further comment.

Various passages from the New Testament that are generally put forth by advocates of munching on the unmunchables will be dealt with under the heading of IS THERE MORE TO THE STORY? in Part III of this book.

5
THE COMMON, THE UNCLEAN, AND THE ABOMINABLE

The particular words used by the Bible in reference to animals whose flesh is prohibited by the dietary laws of the Bible proves to be instructive for the purposes of this study. And, of course, we have in mind the words of the original languages of the Bible, the Hebrew and the Greek, which may receive various translations into our language.

It is commonly the case that the root origins of words in any language have an inescapable literalness to them. For example, "Adam" is a transliteration of the Hebrew letters that spell out the name of the first man to inhabit the earth. The root of that name means reddish, as the color of clay. This is not insignificant, since "God created Adam out of the dust of the ground" (Gen.2:7). Later, the word is used in the generic sense for mankind (Gen.5:2). Working backward then from the generic, we see that all MEN are descended from ADAM whom God created from the EARTH. And so it is that words arise from primitive roots to attain a variety of expanded meanings; literal, figurative, spiritual, etc.

Turning then, to the dietary laws of the Bible, we find that the animals whose flesh man is forbidden to eat, are called "UNCLEAN." Several Hebrew words, related in meaning, translated into English as "unclean" are defined from a Mosaic perspective (that of covenantal ceremonialism), as "foul" in a religious sense; defiled + infamous, polluted, unclean (Strong). The Septuagint, the third century B. C. Greek translation of the Old Testament, which was quoted by the writers of the New Testament, translates the Hebrew word used for the unclean animals of Leviticus 11 and Deuteronomy 14, with the Greek "akathartos," meaning inherently unclean or contaminated, in distinction from "koinos," acquired contamination.

By way of illustration, we could describe a pile of manure as INHERENTLY unclean, meaning that it is by its very nature contaminated. Whereas we would ascribe ACQUIRED contamination to a serving of food that has been dropped on the floor. There is, therefore, a world of difference between the two.

"COMMON" is a frequent translation of both the Hebrew and Greek words that mean "exposed, shared by many; hence ceremonially profane or unholy." Being "common," such things are contaminated or polluted by contact with impurity. They have ACQUIRED an unworthy status by virtue of a contact or transfer of uncleanness from a source beyond their own nature. In the Tabernacle, the show-bread was holy, consecrated or separated unto the LORD. All other bread would then be considered "common," exposed, so to speak, to the world and matters outside the pale of the holy; this in a ceremonial context, of course.

Lastly, "ABOMINATION" is a word used to describe unclean animals, their dead carcasses, and various human sins such as incest, adultery, sacrificing one's seed to Moloch, homosexual acts, beastiality, and sorcery. Several Hebrew words translated in the English Bible as "abomination" mean filth or something disgusting (especially idolatry). The Greek noun used in the Septuagint to translate the Hebrew words for "abomination" is "bdelugma," which means, among other things, an object of moral repugnance; and the verb "bdelusso" means to defile or to loathe. The passage in Leviticus 18:6-30 that applies the word "abomination" to the various sins itemized above, concludes by declaring: "Whoever shall commit any of these abominations, even the souls who commit them shall be cut off from among their people."

And so, it is evident that the abominable unclean animals keep very wicked bedfellows. This alone should cause your fork to freeze midway to your mouth over a platter of unclean meats!

UNCLEAN HANDS IN THE NEW TESTAMENT

The passage in Mark 7:2, where Christ and His disciples are faulted by the Scribes and Pharisees for eating bread with "unclean hands," a violation of the Jews ceremonial tradition, illustrates the use of "koivais" (in other places translated "common") to denote ACQUIRED

CONTAMINATION. Quite literally, washing cleanses dirty hands, hands that have acquired some form of uncleanness. These hands are not by nature inherently contaminated.

As a matter of fact, in modern times we observe the distinction, cleansing things that have acquired contamination and literally destroying things inherently poisonous, such as poison oak, toadstools, etc.

The biblical health and dietary laws recognize this distinction as do the ceremonial laws which are built upon the literal. It is important to note that the ceremonial laws are founded on the very real qualities of physical things. They are not simply arbitrary distinctions between things having no innate qualities of note.

> Beware the common, the unclean,
> and the abominable!

6
THE REST OF THE STORY

In essence, Peter's vision in chapter ten of Acts is saying: "The preaching of the Gospel now goes out to all men without distinction." Peter summed it up well: "God has shown me that I should not call any man common or unclean" (vs.28). "Kill! Eat!" means "evangelize...go teach all nations all my commandments" (Mt:28:20).

Peter's vision signified the inclusion of the elect Gentiles in God's covenant, thus setting them aside from other unbelievers in the matter of their whole life. Those "called" Gentiles were to become God-lovers, the redeemed of the Lamb, who, in every age eat, drink, work, play, think, and do all to the glory of God in faithful obedience to His law-word. They are freed from the bondage of sin, freed from bondage to health-destroying habits, and freed from self-will. For them it is now "Thy will be done"...in MY menu as it is in God's menu!

ACTING LAWFULLY

As the record of the Acts of the Apostles progresses, and Gentiles were more and more drawn into the covenant of Grace (Ac.11:18; 13:12; 14:27), problems arose because of the practices of Gentiles newly admitted to the church. It was complicated by the fact that some of the Pharisees, having believed, insisted that converted Gentiles receive the Older Covenant sign of circumcision.

And so, the church council gathered at Jerusalem, and, having considered the errors of both the Pharisees and the Gentile converts, they sent letters out to the churches in Antioch, Syria, and Cilicia to correct the situation. After first dealing with circumcision, they next addressed the Gentile practices, thus:

For it seemed good to the Holy Spirit and to us to lay on you no greater burden than these necessary things: that you abstain from meats offered to idols, and from blood, and from things strangled, and from fornication; from which, if you keep yourselves, you shall do well. Be prospered (Acts 15: 28-29).

This is a restatement of verse 20 where it says "abstain from pollutions of idols," and in chapter 21 there is further clarification where it is recorded: "...only that they keep themselves from both idol sacrifice[1], and blood, and things strangled, and fornication." From this narrowing of the prohibition it appears that the churches are not just prohibited from eating meats offered to idols, but that it was the entire process that was referred to; offer-

---
1. Grk: eidolothuton

ing meats to idols (which is pollution), and then eating those meats (I Cor. 10:21), and finally, fornicating with temple prostitutes. Corinth, for example, was a city of many pagan temples dedicated to false gods; Apollo, Athena, Poseidon, Askelepios, and Aphrodite, the latter reputed to having been served by one thousand priestess-prostitutes.

Pagan worship was a package deal and the whole package was sinful. The Apostles did right in exhorting the Gentile converts to turn from these wicked practices to a righteous life style.

But before continuing, I Corintians 8 deserves further comment. It may appear to contradict the Jerusalem council's determination on abstention from consuming blood. In fact, Hodge eliminates this supposed difficulty by saying that the prohibition of blood demanded by the council's letter to the churches was but of temporary duration, a view unsupported by other scripture. His outline of the Greek and Roman idolatrous sacrifices, however, is instructive:

"The victims offered in sacrifices were usually divided into three parts. One was consumed on the altar, another was given to the priest,and a third was retained by the offerer. The portion given to the priest, if not needed for himself, was sent to the market. The portion retained by the offerer was either eaten at his own table, or within the precincts of the temple."

Several other things should be noted, in addition to Hodge's description of idolatrous worship, that have bearing on our concerns. 1.) A person could be invited into the outer court of the temple to partake of the feasting without having taken part in the actual worship-sacrifice service. 2.) The assumption that Gentiles sacrificed and ate ONLY unclean animals is erroneous. Bulls were common animals. In fact, in some religions, like Mithraism of the late first century, the only animals they sacrificed were bulls, whose flesh was then shared in a sacred meal. The Romans sacrificed cattle and sheep, clean animals, as well as pigs. 3.) "Blood is the drink of the Gods or the drink shared by mortals with the Gods" (pg.255, the Encyclopedia of Religion, McMillan Pub. Co.). The Jerusalem council condemned the "eating of blood and things strangled [those small animals caught in a snare or hand-strangled]." But the pagans killed the larger animals by slitting their throats and letting them bleed to death, the Hebrew practice, which is quite Kosher. Hence, one could buy and eat from the market-place, meats sacrificed to idols, without consuming blood.

But even more important, is our understanding of the Apostle Paul's comments in I Corinthians eight. Is he contradicting the council's prohibitions, or is there more to the story? The scriptural principle of interpretation that at the mouth of two or three witnesses truth must be established, and also the wisdom in not relying on one obscure or seemingly contradictory passage at the expense of numerous clear ones, deserve consideration at this point. The council's thinking was hardly innovative, having its roots in the Old Testament. Balaam taught Balak (cf. Num.31:16) to put a stumbling block before the sons of Israel, to eat things sacrificed to idols, and to commit fornication (cf. Num. 25). And our Lord, in His letter to the church at Pergamos (Rev.2:12ff), holds it against them that they have in their midst those who, "hold the teachings of Balaam, who taught Balak to cast a stumbling block before the sons of Israel, to eat things sacrificed to idols and to commit fornication." Failure to repent would cause Christ to come upon them quickly in judgment. Here we have two strong witnesses, from both Old and New Testament scriptures, condemning the same things that the Jerusalem council did: EATING THINGS SACRIFICED TO IDOLS AND COMMITTING FORNICATION!

The Apostle Paul's teachings to the Corinthian church then are best grasped in the light of the above and as further exposited by an early twentieth century theologian, H.B. Sweet:

"Writing to Corinth some fifteen years after the council, St. Paul had occasion to argue with Christians who regarded the eating of things sacrificed to idols as a thing indifferent; and though he does not take his stand on the Jerusalem decree, he opposes the practice on the ground that it gave offense to weak brethren (I Cor. 8:4, 9-10), and also because of the connection which he regarded as existing between idol-worship and unclean spirits (I Cor. 10:20: The things that the Gentiles sacrifice, they sacrifice to demons, and not to God; and I do not want you to become sharers in demons; to partake of 'the table of unclean spirits' (I Cor. 10:21) was inconsistent with participation in the Eucharist." - Henry Barclay Sweet, Commentary on Revelation (Grand Rapids: Kregel Publications, {1911} 1977), pp. 37f.

The above considerations cast essential light on the imagined conflict between Paul's writing in I Corinthians eight and the content of the letter sent out by the council at Jerusalem as reported in Acts fifteen. Paul did not contradict the Council's decree, nor did he undo God's dietary laws. May God grant us the grace to overcome and receive the hidden manna for our food and a white stone wherein is written a new name (Rev. 2:17).

PERSEVERING PETER

Almost a quarter of a century after Peter's vision of the sheetful of unclean beasts lowered from heaven, he wrote his epistles, therein evidencing his continued low estimation of the unclean animal kingdom.

In his condemnation of apostates as sinful, adulterous, cursed children of darkness, he quotes Proverbs 26:11: "The dog turned to his own vomit; and, the washed sow to wallowing in the mire"(II Pet.2:22). The pejoratives due the unclean animals are still valid for

Peter at that late date. Did he understand the vision to mean "Eat those filthy critters," or had God shown him that the vision had another meaning, preaching Christ to the Gentiles?

A little earlier, in his first epistle, Peter exhorts his readers to "become holy in conduct, because it is written, 'be holy, for I am holy,'" a direct quote from God out of the dietary laws of the Old Testament. In fact, the Levitical exhortation is sandwiched (if you'll pardon the expression) between the prohibitions against eating swarming things and a general reference to four categories of unclean animals:

And every swarming thing that swarms on the earth shall be an abomination. It shall not be eaten. Anything going on its belly, and any going on all four, and having many feet, every swarming thing that swarms on the earth, you shall not eat them. For they are an abomination. You shall not defile yourselves with any swarming thing that swarms, neither shall you make yourselves unclean with them, so that you should be defiled by them. FOR I AM THE LORD YOUR GOD, AND YOU SHALL SANCTIFY YOURSELVES, AND YOU SHALL BE HOLY, FOR I AM HOLY (emphasis added). Neither shall you defile yourselves with any kind of swarming thing that swarms on the earth. For I am the Lord who brings you out of the land of Egypt to be your God. YOU SHALL THEREFORE BE HOLY, FOR

I AM HOLY (emphasis added). This is the law of the animals, and of the fowl, and of every living creature that moves in the waters, and of every creature that swarms on the earth, to make a difference between the clean and the unclean, and between the beast that may be eaten and the beast that may not be eaten (Leviticus 11:41-47).

Also see Deut. 14:2 and Lev.20:26. These are the only places, among the dietary laws, that the admonition "Be holy, for I am holy" is to be found. And Peter finds it appropriate long after his Acts 10 experience to make this kind of reference.

Further, note the reference to God having brought the Israelites "up out of the land of Egypt"(vs.45). On the occasion of their deliverance, God promised that... "if you will listen to the Lord your God, and you will do that which is right in his sight, and will give ear to his commandments, and keep all his laws, I will put none of these DISEASES (emphasis added) upon you which I have brought upon the Egyptians; for I am the Lord who heals you"(Ex.15:26). Also see Deut.7:15 and Deut. 28:58-63 wherein the curse of the covenant is stipulated against the disobedient, and all the diseases of Egypt are again threatened as punishment.

While any and all covenant breaking will occasion this affliction, it cannot be overlooked that the dietary laws are a prominent part of covenant law, and as such, obedience in keeping them will indeed be a barrier to parasites and bacteria present in the unclean diet of pagan cultures.

The Proverbs say, "The curse causeless shall not come"(Prov.26:2). There is a cause and effect principle in God's creation order that can be ignored only at one's peril. Step off a cliff and you'll be hurt. Drink poison and you'll be hurt. Disobey God and be cursed. Obey God and be blessed. Follow the divinely prescribed diet and escape the evil diseases of a worldly culture's unclean diet.

Those who object to following the biblical dietary laws and attempt to exclude them from the moral sphere need to look at Leviticus 20:22-27:

You shall therefore keep all My statutes and all My judgments, and do them, so that the land where I bring you to live shall not spit you out. And you shall not walk in the ways of the nation which I cast out before you. For they committed all these things, and therefore I hated them. But I have said to you, you shall inherit the land, and I will give it to you to possess it, a land that flows with milk and honey. I am the Lord your God, who has separated you from the nations. And you shall make a difference between clean animals and unclean, and between unclean fowls and clean. And you shall not make your souls hateful by beast, or by fowl, or by any kind of living thing

that creeps on the ground, which I have separated from you as unclean. And you shall be holy to Me. For I the Lord, am holy, and have severed you from the nations, so that you should be mine. A man also or woman that has a familiar spirit, or that is a wizard, shall surely be put to death. They shall stone them with stones. Their blood is on them.

In the above, not only is the command to distinguish between clean and unclean animals yoked with being holy, as God is holy, but the passage concludes with making witchcraft and wizardry capital offenses.

By way of reminder, we have earlier seen how the Apostles did not shrink from prohibiting idolatry, eating blood, and fornication in one breath. But the mixture in one context of dietary prohibitions with morals laws is widespread. For instance, idolatry, unclean animals, sexual sins, and homosexuality are rated as "abomination" in God's sight (Lev.20:10-27).

7
"OH, YUCK!"

"Oh, yuck!" is a common exclamation of revulsion in our day, as often as not, the response to an unsavory menu item. Kids, and all too often, even their fathers, may unjustifiably utter it at the sight of broccoli or cauliflower on their dinner plate. These, however ARE nourishing foods.

The author offers this negative exclamation in this chapter in reference to many of the prohibited "unclean" meats mentioned in the Bible. Indeed, "Oh, yuck" may be putting it too mildly, for we have here, not just something unappetizing, but things that can actually harm the health and imperil the life of the consumer.

First, the human body's metabolism is ill-equipped to handle unclean meats which digest in only three hours. Clean meats, on the other hand, require up to eighteen hours to completely digest. Biochemist Dr. Carey Reams, discovered that unclean meats, such as pork, shellfish, catfish, etc., because they are so rapidly digested, produce extremely high energy levels quickly, which are just as quickly expended. These meats digest so rapidly that the body cannot use the proteins which turn into urea and are dumped into the bloodstream so fast that the kidneys fail to eliminate them. They then build up in the body, causing various disorders (See pp.48-50, Health Guide for Survival by Salem Kirban; also, The Curse Causeless Shall Not Come by Nord Davis).

There follow certain specific examples as well as general observations about the kind of animals that are listed as forbidden.

SWINE

Pork is a good place to start since it ranks high on the menu of our society. It also ranks high on what should be anybody's DANGEROUS food list.

The Tyndale Old Testament Commentary on Leviticus makes this sobering observation: "There is no 'safe' temperature at which pork can be cooked to ensure that parasitic organisms are killed."

Farmers testify that swine will eat anything; urine and fecal matter, dead animals, cancerous growths on other hogs, and so on, ad nausea.

And while it takes cows, having a complex digestive system, over twenty-four hours to digest their vegetarian fare and turn it into flesh, the swine's one stomach takes only about four hours to digest its foul fare.

Forty-two diseases and parasites may be passed from swine to humans, not the least of which is trichinosis (trichinella spiralis). In the flesh of the pig, the Trichinae worms are often so minute and nearly transparent as to evade even the inspector's microscope. Once ingested, the trichinae lodge and thrive in various parts of the human body and may be confused with some fifty ailments;

typhoid fever, arthritis, rheumatism, gall bladder trouble, and even acute alcoholism, to name just a few.

Some years ago, Dr, Manley, an expert on animal diseases, claimed that autopsies showed that one out of three people are infected with trichinosis. And how many deaths are followed by an autopsy? Very few!

In addition to trichinae, pigs also host at least twelve other parasitic worms. Yummy!

A look at the biblical description of unclean animals helps to explain why swine are prone to so many parasites and diseases.

1. Their super-simple digestive system works very rapidly, turning its food into flesh.

2. Its apparently cloven-hoof or foot is not completely separated, above as below. Ellicott's Commentary on the Bible makes this appraisal:

The feet of the pig generally have four toes enclosed in separate hoofs. The two middle hoofs, however are much larger, and are divided by a deep cleft, and hence, to all outward appearances the swine is bisclous {cloven-hoofed}.[1]

It is remarkable that in advance of man's investigation into many aspects of God's creation, God in His Word has spoken the factual truth of the matter, as here

---

1. Lev. 11:3 "Whatsoever is cloven-footed, and entirely separateth the Hoof..." The first rule by which the clean quadruped is to be distinguished, is that the hoofs must be completely cloven or divided above as well as below, or as the parallel passage in Deut. 14:6 has it, "and cleaveth the cleft into two claws." Such is the case in the foot of the ox, the sheep, and the goat, where the hoof is wholly divided below as much as it is above. The foot of the dog, the cat, and the lion, though exhibiting a division into several distinct toes or claws, is contrary to the regulation here laid down, inasmuch as the division is simply on the upperside, the lower side being united by a membrane, and hence the hoof is not 'entirely separate'."

in the matter of a seemingly cloven-hoof that in reality is not completely divided. Man has to walk across the room, open his dresser drawer, and start counting to see how many socks he has in the drawer. God, on the other hand, knows without investigating, for He is the creator and governor of all things from the beginning of the world.[2]

CLEAN FISH

Only fish with scales and fins are permissible menu items, and they largely inhabit surface waters where their scales reflect the sunlight which is shunned by such parasites as leeches and scuds. The bodies of unclean fish are NOT mirror-like. Clean fish have overlapping scales, protecting them from their environment, and tails with which they can propel themselves rapidly. We should not be fooled by certain unclean fish, which give an appearance of having scales, but these are really ridges or widely placed scales that leave skin exposed. Clean fish, suitable for human consumption are albacore, bass, bluefish, bonitos, carp, cod, crappie, flounder, groupers, grunts, haddock, hake, halibut, herring, kingfish, mackerel, minnow, pickerel, pike, perch, pollack, redfish, rockfish, salmon, sardine, shad, smelt, snapper, sole, trout, wite fish. etc.[3]

---

2. An illustration by Cornelius Van Til in his writings on Christian apologetics.

3. Harold Hemenway, *Are the Food Laws Scientific*, 1996, pp.19-25. Available from Harold Hemenway for $2.00 at Box 88401, Seattle, Wa., 98188.

SHELLFISH

The requirement of fins and true scales, while ruling out a number of fish, totally excludes what is generally designated as SHELLFISH, whether mollusc (snails, clams, etc.), or crustaceans (lobsters,shrimps, crabs, wood lice, water fleas, and barnacles), and cetaceous animals (mostly marine animals including whales, dolphins, porpoises, etc.)

Shellfish are immobile or slow moving bottom dwellers, eating to a large degree, what comes to them in the way of settling excrement from fish, and dead and decaying animal and plant life, as well as sewage. Shellfish carry a variety of maladies; hepatitis virus, human fecal bacteria and paralytic shellfish poisoning, as well as typhoid fever and intestinal infections.

UNCLEAN FISH

Harold Hemenway, who in his book, Are the Food Laws Scientific, goes into a lot of detail, lists these as unclean water creatures that God calls an abomination: abalone, catfish (bottom fish), clam, crab, crayfish, cuttle fish, dolphin, eel, jellyfish, limpet,lobster, marlin, mussel, octopus, otter, oyster, paddlefish, scallop, sculpins, seal, shark, shrimp, starfish, sticklebacks, sturgeon, squid, walrus, whale, etc.

THE FOWLS OF THE AIR

Leviticus 11:13 calls them abominable and simply lists them by name, not description. It was left up to man to study these creatures to determine their structure and eating habits. At the time of the second temple the Jews formulated a list of rules, descriptive of the unclean fowls: (1) they snatch their food in the air and devour it without first dropping it on the ground; (2) they strike with their talons and press down with their foot the prey to the ground, and then tear off pieces with their beak; (3) when standing on a branch they place two toes of the same foot on one side and two on the other, and not three in front and one behind; (4) their eggs are equally narrow or equally round at both ends, and have the white in the middle and the yolk around it. A few representative fowls are discussed below.

THE EAGLE eats carrion when it is still fresh, but nevertheless dead.

THE BLACK VULTURE (OSSIFRAGE) quite literally "the bone-breaker," because, from high altitude it drops the bones of animals, which other birds of prey have denuded of flesh, upon rocks, to break them open and have access to marrow or render bone fragments more digestible.

THE BLACK VULTURE (OSPREY OR SEA EAGLE) feeds mostly on fish, but will also eat birds and other animals. It also devours the most putrid carrion.

KITES, VULTURES, FALCONS are birds of prey who also like garbage and offal. Vultures are bald so that they won't muss up their "hair" when they plunge their heads into carcasses to eat the entrails.

THE RAVEN eats putrid corpses (Prov. 30:17) and is especially eager to pick out the eyes of the dead, and sometimes even attacks the eyes of the living. "Every raven after its kind" indicates that the whole genus of ravens is intended; the rook, the crow, the jackdaw, the jay, etc.

This incomplete but representative list of the fowls should suffice to show that they are voracious predators and scavengers with no redeeming traits, humanly speaking. Of course, it should be obvious that they have their place in nature, being to a large degree God's flying garbage cans, intended to clean up the environment. In fact, we could call them THE CREATOR'S ENVIRONMENTALISTS!

FLYING SWARMING CREATURES

"Every flying swarming creature going on all four, it is an abomination to you" (Lev.11:20). Perhaps better rendered, all creeping things which have wings. These belong to the fourth class of the Hebrew division of the animal kingdom, which includes all insects. The phrase "going on all four" does not refer to the exact number of feet, but is a manner of speech (as in some modern languages "he was on all fours") for going about in a horizontal position, as opposed to birds who stand upright upon two legs (Ellicott). All of these are forbidden, having varied diets, but some notably pierce and suck blood.

Locusts or grasshoppers are an exception to the rule in this category. "...those which have legs above their feet, to leap with on the earth"(Lev.11:21), that is, those which have the third or hindermost pair of legs much longer and stronger than other insects, and the second joint much larger and stronger, enabling it to leap high into the air. Not noted in the text is the fact that they are vegetarian and have what amounts to four stomachs; a crop, a gizzard, gastric caeca, and a stomach, from front to back. In other words, they, like completely cloven-hoofed beasts, have a complicated digestive system.

Somewhat deficient in vitamin content, they contain up to 50% protein, 20% fat, with mineral salts and some calories. Thus, they are sufficient for survival living when eaten along with honey, as evidenced in the case of John the Baptist dwelling in the wilderness (Mat 3:4).

THE SWARMING THINGS

"And whatever goes on its paws..." that is, animals whose feet are not divided into two parts, but which have feet with fingers like a hand, such as the bear, ape, wolf, cat, etc. These are mostly carnivores. The weasel, for instance, is an extremely voracious creature of prey that kills animals of prey even bigger than itself. It is fond of chickens, and, having pointed and crooked teeth, it can pierce the skull and brain of hens. It has been known to attack sleeping children and to devour human corpses. "Pop, goes the weasel...oh. yuck!"

Rodents also come under this classification. Mice, the great destroyer of crops and carriers of disease. The deadly killer of millions in Europe and Britain, the Bubonic Plague, is spread to humans by fleas from infected rats.

A variety of lizards (reptiles) are also listed here.

SNAKES AND MULTI-FOOTED CRITTERS

"Anything going on its belly, and any going on all four, and all having many feet, even every swarming thing that swarms on the earth, you shall not eat them. For they are an abomination" (Lev.11:42).

Most serpents swallow their prey alive with guts full of yuck; some first constrict it and swallow the dead carcass. They suffer from parasites and have a super-simple digestive system.

Scorpions and beetles are those going on all four. Those having many feet are caterpillars, centipedes, millipedes, etc. Oh, yuck again!

This is not a complete documentary by any means, but you definitely cannot escape the idea that God did not arbitrarily choose some as clean and others as unclean. It wasn't like a flip of the coin; heads up, you're clean; tails, you're unclean. These animals are creatures that God created with a purpose in this world. Many are scavengers who clean up the environment, and all play a part in the balance of nature.

At the completion of His creation, God said that it was good (Gen.1:31). The unclean beasts are GOOD garbage collectors and keep things in balance. Other foods God "created to be received with thanksgiving by those who believe and know the truth. For every creation of God is good"(I Tim.4:3,4). God did not create the unclean with the purpose of being received for human consumption. God doesn't change. His law hasn't changed. The animal world has not changed. There is a great biblically fixed gulf between the clean and the unclean animals.

I am indebted to Ellicott's Commentary on the Whole Bible (4 vol.), 1970 for much of the information contained in this chapter.

PART 3

THE CREATION KEY

8
THE CREATION KEY

THE CREATOR-CREATURE DISTINCTION

We began examining this subject matter, by design, with Peter's vision in Acts ten, only because many Christians today think that the dietary laws of the Bible were abrogated at that point in time. But as we have seen, such is by no means the case. It therefore now behooves us to start at the beginning, at God's creation of the heavens and the earth.

Unlike the many other man-made religions of the world, the bogus faiths whose end is only great disappointment and eternal destruction, biblical faith makes a sharp distinction between the Creator and His creation. God is infinite and eternal, without beginning or end (I Kings 8:27; Ps.139:7-10; 90:2), and what He has created[1] is finite and time-bound. God is not the same as what He has made. God is a spirit, infinite, eternal, and unchangeable, in his being, wisdom, power, holiness,

---

1. The Hebrew verb "bara" of the Genesis one creation account occurs only 55 times in the Old Testament, and it means to create something new as to form and/or matter. The ordinary word for "to make" is "asah", which occurs over 2600 times, and designates the Providential works of God within time and history, not His creative works. God created all things out of nothing by fiat; He spoke and they all came into existence (Gen. 1:3ff; Heb.11:3).

justice, goodness, and truth. There is no cross-over, mingling, or migration from one to the other, nor will there ever be. This, in stark contrast to the absorption of all into one great spirit-being so foolishly held by the "chain-of-being" eastern religions.

THE CREATOR-COVENANTER

While God is transcendent and totally distinct from His creation, "You Lord are high above all the earth"(Ps.97:9), He is also immanent, "Thou art with me"(Ps.23:4). He is everywhere (Prov. 15:3). And the only way that God relates to His creation is by covenant, not by any joining of substance or being, and a covenant relationship is one of law (Deut. 4:13). Covenants are of two major divisions; natural and spiritual, with the universe and with man (Isa.24:4-6). In the case of the latter, a covenant has been defined as "a mutually binding compact between God and His people, sovereignly transacted by the Lord, wherein a promise is made by God which calls for trust on the part of His people, and entails obligations of submission which are sanctioned by blessings and curses" (Greg Bahnsen, By This Standard, I.C.E. Tyler, Tx.1985, p.353). By the Covenant of Redemption, the eternal Godhead decreed that Christ would die for God's elect people, freeing them from the curse of sin and giving them life eternal (Acts 2:23; I Peter 1:1-8). God's covenant with the material universe is of a different nature although linked to His covenant with man. That is, as goes man, so goes the universe. It was by

man's disobedience that nature was cursed (Gen. 3:14-19).
One further thing needs to be said before moving on. Man was created in God's spiritual image and commanded to exercise dominion over all of creation (Gen.1:26-28). He promptly began this task by naming (classifying) the animal kingdom (Gen.2:19-20). With Adam's fall, the image of God in him was marred, so that without regeneration of his soul his rule over creation is quite defective, yet he is still commanded to rule (Gen.9:1-7). Christians, of course, being renewed in the image of Christ (Ep.4:22-24), are especially well-equipped to do this. It is a part of that obedience to Christ, in exercising biblical dominion, to ascertain what is a proper diet for care and maintenance of the Christian's body which is essential to evangelizing the world and caring for the natural order. And the means to define that proper diet are to be found in the Word of God and careful study of the animal and plant kingdoms. That is what this book is all about.

GOD'S COVENANT OF DAY AND NIGHT

There is a divinely established order in every aspect of the universe. Were it a chance universe, as popularly held by many, nobody could predict anything. Science would be impossible, technology an ever-disappointing dream, and life itself would be an impossibility. No creation-order...only chaos and death.
"Thus saith the Lord; If ye can break my covenant of

the day, and my covenant of the night, and that there should not be day and night in their season; Then may also my covenant be broken with David my servant, that he should not have a son to reign upon his throne" (Jeremiah 33:20-21).

We might paraphrase this promise thus: "God's covenant with David is so sure that it could only be broken if man could disrupt the creation law-order, the day and night cycle." While the primary thrust of Jeremiah gives immeasurable hope to those who trust in God, it also shows us that the material universe is ordered with regularity by its Creator, a regularity that extends to every God-created fact. We can depend on day to follow night, that seasons will always follow in order, the laws of physics, chemistry, electronics, logic, etc. are consistent and dependable. The genetics of organic creatures is such that they produce "after their kind" (Genesis 1:11-12); every animal reproduces after its kind (Genesis 1:24); oaks do not sometimes produce oaks and at other times pine or palm trees. Cattle don't have cats or dogs, etc. Every "clean" and "unclean" animal was created with certain characteristics and for a purpose decreed by its Creator. They are what they are because that is the way God created them, and that is the way they continue to this day; some carnivorous and others vegetarian; some parasitic and others not; some are scavengers who clean up the world and others are not. Some were created with very simple digestive systems and others have complicated digestive tracts. Some are meant to be a part of man's diet and others are not! The same may be said for plant life.

THE VEGETARIAN DIET

Vegetables and fruits fit for human consumption are plentiful, yet on the whole they are in the minority. God either directly revealed to Adam what plants were edible or Adam had to find out through experimentation. Remember, he had to "name" (define) the animal kingdom. Some produce are not readily digested and some are poisonous. Whether or not God gave our first parents specifics in this realm, we cannot be sure. However, the biblical record does contain a basic guideline; "And God said, Behold! I have given you every herb bearing seed...and every tree which has in it the fruit of a tree yielding seed...to you it shall be for food" (Genesis 1:29). ONLY plants that reproduce by SEED are on the human diet. Thus, by omission, excluded are such parasites as the mushroom that reproduces by spore, not seed. And many of these varieties are poisonous.

THE MEAT DIET

After the fall, when God clothed Adam and Eve with animal skins, meat was included in his diet, but not blood or fat (Lev. 3:17).

"Abel brought an offering of the firstborn of his flock" (Gen.4:4). Abel had a "flock", not a herd of "swine". There is mention only of sheep, cattle, certain birds, and fish as man's fare.

After several thousand years, Noah was commanded by God to take aboard his ark representatives of the two major divisions of animal life, the clean and the unclean (Gen.7:2). Apparently Noah, and all mankind, already knew one from the other. Noah needed no description of them. And after the flood Noah made burnt offerings to the Lord of CLEAN animals and birds (Gen.8:20). God wanted only the best in the way of sacrifice, and it would have been little sacrifice to offer a beast that God regarded as "unclean" and "abominable," and hateful to Him. From the beginning God has given only the best to man for a diet.

However, the unclean were and are "good" in a context other than human consumption. They are the scavengers of nature, and others play an important role in the balance of nature, yet are not suitable for the human diet, either for digestive reasons and/or because they carry parasites, bacteria, viruses, and also because, as in the case of swine, their flesh is too rapidly digested for human metabolism. Others, like shellfish, rich in a few minerals, are prone to be laden with pollution. They are the vacuum cleaners of the coastal river-dumping grounds.

THE ARK'S CARGO

Unclean meat advocates are quick to point out that Noah was given great gastronomical liberty by God: "Every moving thing that lives shall be food for you"(Gen.9:3), and by omission of mentioning the CLEAN and UNCLEAN distinction of the animals taken aboard the ark (Gen.7:2-3), they fall into the out-of-context trap. Let's illustrate this in a different frame of reference. A man stores apples and pears in his cellar. There is also a clearly marked canister of rat poison in his cellar. The man tells his son that he may eat whatever he finds in the cellar. Context tells us that the rat poison is not an option intended or presented to the son. The son, even if he were the prince of dullards, would not interpret the father's command to include the rat poison.

THE MOSAIC COVENANT

With the advent and administration of the Mosaic covenant, about 1450 B.C., we see the formal codified institution of laws established at creation in an upgraded framework, a covenantal framework, that is refined and adapted to the nation Israel. This national code encompassed all of life for the God-lover. We do not see new laws per se, but we see them formalized and fleshed-out in greater detail. The entire law of God was then ratified as the constitution for the nation Israel, which nation in all respects, civil and religious, was then covenanted to serve Jehovah (Ex. 24:3-8). Much earlier, about 2000 B.C., God said that "Abraham obeyed my voice and kept my charge, my statutes, my commandments, and my laws (Gen.26:4,5).

In the Mosaic era we find that the moral laws of God,

written on man's heart since the beginning (Ro.2:15), were then etched in stone (Ex.24:12), and penned in case law detail in lengthy covenant documents such as the book of Deuteronomy. These include the dietary laws that divide God's health food from the junk food of the world, the latter, perhaps better described on the whole, as God's environmental garbage cans.

The passing of the Mosaic era was curtains for national Israel, but not for God's laws of health and morality (Mt. 5:17-20). These laws have always been universal in scope and they continue so (Jer. 50:14; I Tim. 1:8-10). To flaunt them is to despise God's righteous reign and governance of our lives.

9
IS THERE MORE TO THE STORY?

A number of New Testament passages are seized upon by friends of the unclean diet as supportive of their position, but upon careful examination they prove not to rank even as seasoning for prairie dog stew. The first of these is the fourteenth chapter of the Epistle to the Romans.

ROMANS XIV

1 And receive him who is weak in the faith, but not to judgments of your thoughts.
2 For indeed one believes to eat all things; but being weak, another eats vegetables.
3 Do not let him who eats despise him who does not eat; and do not let him who does not eat judge him who eats, for God has received him.
4 Who are you that judges another's servant? To his own master he stands or falls. But he will stand, for God is able to make him stand.
5 One indeed esteems a day above another day; and another esteems every day alike. Let each one be fully assured in his own mind.
6 He who regards the day regards it to the Lord; and he not regarding the day, does not regard it to the

Lord. He who eats, eats to the Lord, for he gives God thanks; and he who does not eat, does not eat to the Lord, and gives God thanks.

7 For none of us lives to himself, and no one dies to himself.

8 For both if we live, we live to the Lord; and if we die, we die to the Lord. Therefore both if we live, and if we die, we are the Lord's.

9 For this Christ both died and rose and lived again, that he might be Lord both of the dead and living.

10 But why do you judge your brother? Or why do you despise your brother? For all stand before the judgment seat of Christ.

11 For it is written, "As I live, says the Lord, every knee shall bow to Me, and every tongue shall confess to God."

12 So then each one of us will give an account concerning himself to God.

13 Then let us not judge one another any more, but rather judge this, not to put a stumbling-block or an offense toward his brother.

14 I know and am persuaded in the Lord Jesus, that nothing by itself is common; except to him who esteems anything to be common, it is common.

15 But if your brother is grieved with your food, you no longer walk according to love. Do not with your food destroy him for whom Christ died.

16 Then do not let your good be spoken evil of,

17 for the kingdom of God is not eating and drinking, but righteousness and peace and joy in the Holy

Spirit.
18 For he who serves Christ in these things is well-pleasing to God, and approved by men.
19 So then let us pursue the things of peace, and the things for building up one another.
20 Do not undo the work of God for food. Truly, all things indeed are clean, but it is bad to the man eating because of a stumbling-block.
21 It is good neither to eat flesh, not to drink wine, nor anything by which your brother stumbles, or is offended, or is made weak.
22 Do you have faith? Have it to yourself before God. Blessed is he who does not condemn himself in what he approves.
23 But, the one doubting, if he eats, he has been condemned, because it is not of faith; and all that is not of faith is sin.

    The chapter begins with the comparison of one who "believes to eat all things; but being weak, another eats vegetables." This is obviously a contrast between vegetarians and meat-eaters, having no reference in this context to unclean meats.

    Initially we must address presupposition and context here, the former sets the stage, and the latter is interpreted by the former. That is, by way of example, if my presupposition is that all Englishmen are gentlemen, and I declare that Sherlock Holmes was an Englishman, then it is assumed that he was a gentleman. In a dietary context, if the presupposition is that only clean foods are edible, and I state that I eat all things, then it may be safely assumed that by eating "all" things I eat from the entire menu of CLEAN things, and not that I indiscriminately eat both clean and unclean, for to do so would be claiming to eat the inedible, a denial of my presupposition.

Therefore, those who by error, misreading and misinterpretation, prejudice, and what-have-you, reach the erroneous conclusion that the unclean meats are wholesome and that their temporary status among ceremonial prescriptions has expired, have as their presupposition that, quite literally, ANY and ALL animal flesh is fit for human consumption. Hence, holding to that presupposition as a matter of faith, it is not surprising that almost every reference to food and diet in the New Testament is cast into the mold prepared for it from the very foundation of the Yuck-is-yummy philosophy.

Verse fourteen of Romans 14 deserves our careful attention:

"...nothing by itself is COMMON (Greek; "koinon"-acquired contamination) except to him who esteems anything to be common, it is common." Understanding from our prior study of this word, the basis for a "common" rating is that it has been exposed, thereby acquiring contamination. In opposition to this is the word "akatharov" which has the meaning of inherent contamination. With this as a foundation for its use in the vegetarian's vocabulary we can reach an intelligent understanding of this passage. Meat has an acquired negativity which is imposed upon it by the vegetarian's outlook. He sees meat as undesirable for any number of reasons; it is cruel to slaughter and eat animals, animals are part of the chain-of-being of all life, flesh is not readily digested, it ferments in the bowels, etc. In the vegetarian's eyes, meat is a no-no. Meat has acquired an ignoble reputation, imposed on it from outside itself, from the vegetarian's mindset. "Nothing by itself is COMMON!"

Similarly, in verse five:"One indeed esteems a day above another day; and another esteems every day alike." To esteem is to place a value on something. Again, the idea of an acquired characteristic, placed on something from without.

The general idea presented in Romans fourteen is the doctrine of Christian liberty. Practically speaking, many things fall into that realm of the adiaphora, things indifferent. Shall I wear a green or a blue tie? Shall we hold our dinner party in candlelight or by electric lighting? Or, as in the instant case, shall I eat meat or be a vegetarian? Shall I esteem one day more important than another? And the conclusion of the Apostle, tempered with Christian love, is that for the sake of our brother, we will not make an issue of such matters. We shall not offend him in something that is really inconsequential.

On an issue of principle, of biblical ethics, we cannot waver, however. I will not cease from public worship because my brother holds that true worship, being that of spirit and truth, can take place only in the solitude of one's soul, perhaps on a high mountain or out on the desert. ONLY on optional matters do we have any freedom of choice.

This is the context of Romans fourteen, not the dietary laws of Leviticus eleven and Deuteronomy fourteen, which are enduring laws of God's creation, not one jot or tittle of which will pass away as long as the world exists (Mt.5:17-20).

Verse twenty, in continuance of the doctrine of Christian liberty, reminds the reader that the vegetarian diet vs. the meat diet is still the subject under discussion, when it says: "Do not undo the work of God for food. Truly, all things indeed are clean, but it is bad to the man eating because of a stumbling-block. It is good neither to eat flesh, nor drink wine, nor anything by which your brother stumbles, or is offended, or is made weak." The language itself turns stronger by way of emphasis to declare that, "all things indeed are clean," here using the Greek "katharov" rather than "koinon," and the repeated reference to flesh eating coupled with wine drinking; for truly, a diet of clean meat and a moderate use of wine are permitted by Scripture. "All things are clean" compares favorably to the instruction given Noah: "Every moving thing that lives shall be food for you"(Gen.9:3). The context there, being that of the dietary distinction between the clean and the unclean animals taken aboard the ark (Gen.7:2).

Such contexts are not rare in the Bible. When Jesus said, "I will draw all men unto me"(John 12:32), he cannot mean universalism, for it must be in the context of "The good shepherd lays down his life for the sheep"(John 10:11), while there are others who are NOT of his sheep (John 10:26). The "all" are His sheep, (not the goats) His elect, known unto Him from the foundation of the world (Ep.2:4-5; Ro.8:28-30; 9:14-18; I Tim.2:5-6).

I TIMOTHY 4:1-5

**1 The Spirit expressly says that in the latter times some shall depart from the faith, giving heed to seducing spirits and teachings of demons,
2 speaking lies in hypocrisy, being seared in their own conscience,
3 forbidding to marry, saying to abstain from foods which God has created to be received with thanksgiving by those who believe and know the truth.
4 For every creation of God is good, and nothing to be refused if it is received with thanksgiving.
5 For it is sanctified through the word of God and prayer.**

Here, Paul warns Timothy of the asceticists, those who forbid to marry and require abstention from certain foods. Actually, this passage STRENGTHENS the validity of keeping the dietary laws. First, we must ask, what foods has God created to be received with thanksgiving? The CLEAN meats is the obvious, creation-founded answer. The unclean were NOT created for man to eat. The clean meats were created to be received with thanksgiving by those who BELIEVE and KNOW THE TRUTH! These are the ones accepting God's Old Testament laws as true and binding...they believe and know the truth (vs. 3).

Every creation of God is good (vs.4). This we know from Genesis one, but the crux of the whole matter centers on the purpose of those various created good things. Some are good to eat and others are not. The "unclean" animals are good in their own sphere, that of cleaning up the environment and keeping a balance in the natural realm.

Verse five reaffirms this: "for it is SANCTIFIED through the word of God and prayer." Sanctified means "set apart," as well is the case with the "clean" animals; they are set apart through the word of God as things suitable for human consumption (Lev.11; Deut.14).

However, this passage's primary concern is with refuting vegetarianism and celibacy as practices of piety. The unclean flesh protagonists impose their own presupposition upon it to champion their cause.

COLOSSIANS 2:20-23

This passage is alleged to encroach on the necessity of observing the dietary laws. Let's look at it analytically and in context:

20 If then you died with Christ from the elements of the world, why, as though living in the world, are you subject to its ordinances:
21 touch not, taste not, handle not -
22 which things are all for corruption in the using, according to the commands and doctrines of men?

23 These things indeed have a reputation of wisdom in will-worship and humility, and neglecting of the body, not in any honor for the satisfying of the flesh.

Highlighting just a few words quickly demolishes this passage as an opponent of dietary conformity. Verse twenty-two tells us that it is the "elements" and the "ordinances" of the "WORLD" that we must guard against, not GOD'S ordinances. Those regulations herein listed; "touch not, taste not, handle not" have no reference to God's dietary laws...they are the commandments and doctrines of MEN!

I CORINTHIANS 6:12

Paul's declaration: "All things are lawful to me" is another playground for antinomians of every stripe, and especially those who champion the cause of lawlessness by Scripture-twisting. Paul's statement comes in the narrow context of an evaluation of things indifferent. It is not a reference to things absolutely forbidden by Scripture...immoral acts or consumption of unclean meats, for he adds: "But I will not be brought under the power of any," a rejection of the mind-control that pietists (who are usually legalists) crave to impose on others.

Unclean meats are prohibited without any New Testament qualification or abrogation, and as such, do not fall under the cloak of Christian liberty. They are not things indifferent!

Again, it is like saying: "Christ died for all men," meaning all of God's elect, the reprobate not even coming under consideration. All things were lawful for the Apostle Paul. Yes, all things LAWFUL are truly lawful. To say that all UNLAWFUL things are lawful is to destroy reason, enthrone contradiction, and invite chaos into all of life.

MARK 7:14-23

14 And calling near all the crowd, He said to them, Listen to me, every one of you, and understand.
15 There is nothing from outside a man which entering into him can defile him. But the things which come out of him, those are the ones that defile the man.
16 If anyone has ears to hear, let him hear.
17 And when He had entered into the house away from the crowd, His disciples asked Him concerning the parable.
18 And He said to them, are you also without understanding? Do you not perceive that whatever enters into the man from outside cannot defile him,
19 because it does not enter into his heart, but into the belly, and goes out into the wastebowl, purifying all food?
20 And He said. That which comes out of the man is what defiles the man.
21 For from within, out of the heart of men, proceed evil thoughts, adulteries, fornications, murders, thefts, covetousness, wickedness, deceit, lasciviousness, an

evil eye, blasphemy, pride, foolishness.
23 All these evil things pass out from inside and defile the man.

Here we have a discussion revolving around the source of man's defilement. It is a very simple proposition—men are not defiled by what enters from the outside, but by what proceeds from their hearts. From within the fallen nature of men, out of their souls, springs forth every manner of sin. As sin goes, it is not what you eat, but how your heart speaks to all the issues of life.

Some texts, such as the NIV, contain a statement tacked onto the last verse of this text: "(In saying this, Jesus declared all foods 'clean.')" This sentence is not found in the Textus Receptus, the mass of over 5000 Greek manuscripts copied from the original documents, then recopied and recopied by the early churches growing up in the major sweep of Gospel proclamation and expansion, and from which the complete text of the New Testament that we have today was derived.

Ellicott's Commentary on the Whole Bible takes this notice of the addition to the text: "It is a possible conjecture that the words 'cleansing all meats' may have been, at first, a marginal note... attached to 'He saith,' and have afterwards found their way into the text."

In other words, somebody, in times past, has been tampering with the Word of God! For a very brief overview of the textual problems imposed upon us by ancient heretics and their modern counterparts, unbelieving scholars and their dupes, see the article in the

Appendix, titled WILL THE REAL BIBLE PLEASE STAND UP.

PART 4

THE NEW CREATION

10
THE NEW HEAVENS AND THE NEW EARTH

A general misconception prevails in Christendom, due largely to "end-time" preachers who predict the coming of Christ at any moment, either to usher in a Jewish millennium ruled by Christ from Jerusalem, or to end history with the commencement of the eternal state. This writer is confident that these teachers and their followers are dreadfully misdirected in their interpretation of the Scriptures. It is not the purpose of this book to deal with this subject in great detail, but the truth of the matter needs to be brushed-in with a few broad strokes at this time because it does have some bearing on this subject matter.

Old Testament imagery for the end of kingdoms and cultures is painted in astronomical colors; the darkening or falling of sun, moon, and stars (Isa.13:10; 34:4; Ezek.32:7; Joel 2:28-32). God's coming in judgment is also graphically portrayed as His riding or coming in the clouds (Isa.19:1; Ps.97:2,3; 104:3;Nah. 1:3).

The New Testament picks up all these figures in its warnings of the impending wrath of God upon apostate Israel. This is especially true in Christ's Olivet discourse (Mt.24; Mk. 13; Lu.21), where such heavenly disruptions speak of the coming destruction of Jerusalem in A.D. 70 by the Romans. There is, prophetically and figuratively speaking, a passing away of the old heavens and the old earth, that is, the end of Israel as God's chosen nation. It is lights out for a disobedient people, and lights on for the New Israel, a people that God calls to Himself from every nation and people and tongue (Ro. 2:28,29; 11:1-32; Ps.22:27,28).

The new heavens and the new earth are picturesque figures of the advent of God's new covenant rule over His people and His creation, during which He progressively lifts His curse. This is initially a spiritual redemption, that in its outworkings encompasses and changes all things, body and soul, institutions and nations. Redeemed men are busy redeeming time, matter, and space. They are God's tools to extend His kingdom internationally by the preaching of the Gospel (Isa. 52:10, 13-15; 60:3; Mt.28:18-20). The righteous Word of God gives direction to every sphere of life. Changed are personal relations, the rule of nations, and everything in between, not the least of which is DIET!

The Bible promises widespread blessings to the covenant-keeping nation, and His curses weigh heavily upon national covenant-breaking (Deut. 7:9-11; 28:1-64). So, in the maturing Messianic reign of Christ from heaven, the world will more and more be brought under the rule of God's law, and as a consequence, more and more blessed (Isa.11:9), until men again attain longevity comparable to that of the patriarchs: "There shall be no more an infant of days, nor an old man that hath not fulfilled his days, for the child shall die a hundred years old, but the sinner being a hundred shall be cursed"(Isa.65:20). Please take heed, this is NOT the ETERNAL state...DEATH still takes its toll. And sinners, while not abounding, are still around, albeit they engage in their forbidden fare secretly: "a people who remain among the graves, and sleep in tombs, who eat swine's flesh, and broth from hateful things in their vessels; who say keep to yourself, do not come near me; for I am holier than you"(Isa.65:4,5). This, in the time of New Heavens and a New Earth (Isa.65:17; II Co.5:17; Rev.21:5). God's word goes on to describe sinners in that period. They will persevere in their perversity: "Those who sanctify themselves, and purify themselves to go into the gardens, behind one tree in the middle, eating swine's flesh,and the hateful thing, and the mouse, will be cut off together, says the Lord"(Isa.66:17). How very interesting, that in the beginning sin irrupted under a tree of forbidden fruit, and near the end of sin's reign there will still be those whose god is their belly, hiding under a tree.

The appetites of men will be sanctified by God's laws of diet; no unclean meat, no fat or blood, no scavenger beasts and no scavenger organs from any beast. Nor will men partake of parasitic (and sometimes poisonous) plants such as mushrooms. Finally, man's belly will not be his god! God's word will rule both mind and body! And man will delight in clean meats, and a balanced and nutritious diet, with moderation tempering all!

11
GOD'S DIET FOR MODERN MAN

"As the bird by wandering, as the swallow by flying, so the curse causeless shall not come" (Proverbs 26:2).

THE CURSE CAUSELESS SHALL NOT COME

Proverbs 26:2 tells us that we live in a cause and effect universe. Man is cursed or blessed in this world in a cause and effect manner in accord with his obedience or lack thereof to the natural laws of the universe as well as the prescriptive or revealed will of God as expressed in his law-word.

Step from a high cliff and you suffer destruction, having violated the law of gravity. Die in your sins (the violation of God's moral laws) and you will suffer eternal punishment. These concepts seem pretty clear cut. And the matter of the health of your body—diet, exercise, rest—should be equally clear, except that we tend to have a cultural veil over our eyes in many ways. Fast foods, soft drinks, lifeless and highly processed foods grown on soil depleted of natural organic nutrients, and consumption of unclean meats, all have negative effects on our health. The results of such abuses of the human body are largely responsible for the degenerative diseases that plague western society today: cancer, heart and vascular disease, stroke, arthritis, tooth and gum disease, hypoglycemia, diabetes, ulcers, parasites, and allergies are caused largely by diet. Parasites are also becoming recognized as being numerous and destructive to our health. A return to a clean meat diet and natural foods with full nutrient value is a must for everybody who wants to be healthy and have a long and productive life.

To assist you in your desire to be "more than conquerors" and to "glorify God in your BODY and in your spirit," what follows is submitted for your consideration.

TEN COMMANDMENTS FOR A HEALTHY BODY

1. Read the Bible every day and follow God's dietary laws as given in Leviticus 11 and Deuteronomy 14. Also, heed the various sanitation precautions of God's Word.

2. Eliminate refined white sugar, substituting raw sugar, unfiltered honey, or real maple sugar.

3. Eliminate white flour and refined grain products, substituting whole wheat flour and other whole grain products.

4. Eliminate refined white common table salt. Use gray natural salt (Celtic, from France-very best) or Real Salt (mined and unrefined) extremely high in natural minerals, pinkish in color (from Utah).

These salts are available at your local health food store.

5. Eliminate refined oils; shortening, lard, and hydrogenated products, such as hydrogenated peanut butter and margarine. Substitute unrefined, cold pressed oil (canola, olive, or flax seed), real butter, and old fashioned (natural) peanut butter without additives.

6. Eliminate, if possible, pasteurized homogenized milk, and substitute certified raw milk or cultured milk products. Yogurt that is sugar free and honey sweetened is available at health food stores.

7. Eliminate canned, cooked frozen foods and vegetables, substituting fresh and dehydrated foods. Fifty percent of your diet should be raw and well balanced with roughage.

8. Eliminate food products containing chemical additives and preservatives, the most common being BHA, BHT, sodium nitrate, and calcium propinate. Read the labels—the enemies are numerous.

9. Eliminate coffee, tea, cocoa, soft drinks (including those containing artificial sweeteners), and substitute any of a host of herb teas, and fresh fruit and vegetable juices.

10. You must further supplement your diet with vitamins, minerals, enzymes, etc. derived from natural sources and without added preservatives, etc.

And of course, there is the eleventh commandment; get plenty of rest and exercise that brings forth perspiration. Walking around the house or the office isn't it.

"As the bird by wandering, as the swallow by flying, so the curse causeless shall not come" (Proverbs 26:2).

– Jean M. Lockman

****

FREE! FREE! FREE! FREE! FREE!

For a free cassette tape with information
on nutrition, write to my son,
DAVID LOCKMAN
233 Rogue River Highway, Suite 13
Grants Pass, Oregon 97527

APPENDIX

FOOD IMAGES IN DREAMS AND VISIONS

Peter's Vision in Acts X

God showed Peter that his vision of an unclean beast-bearing sheet let down from heaven and accompanied by the command to kill and eat meant that he was to call no man unclean, and that he was therefore to preach the Gospel to the Gentiles (Acts 10).

Egyptian Dreams

The dreams of Pharoah's cup-bearer and baker, who were in prison with Joseph in Egypt, had a different meaning than a literal interpretation would indicate.

The cup-bearer dreamed of ripe grapes from three branches that he squeezed into Pharoah's cup. The interpretation: he was to be restored to his job in three days.

The baker dreamed that birds ate food out the top basket of three resting upon his head. The interpretation: he was to be executed in three days.

Both dreams, centering on food consumption, meant something entirely different; 1.) freedom and a job, 2.) the death penalty.

The Barley Cake

Gideon's dream of a cake of barley bread rolling into a Midian tent had nothing to do with food or eating, but signified a military victory over the Midianites (Judges 7:13-15).

The Boiling Pot

Jeremiah's vision of a boiling pot was unrelated to soup or stew. It forecast the invasion of Judah by a foe from the north (Jeremiah 1:13-16).

Reader's Digest

Ezekiel ate a book, but it had to do with coming weepings, mourning, and woe, not a papyrus diet (Ezekiel 2:8ff).

The Apostle John ate a little book that meant he would prophesy before many peoples, nations, tongues, and kings (Rev.10:9-11).

Picnic Nix

Jehovah's vision given to Amos of a basket of summer fruit signified judgment on Israel, not a picnic (Amos 8:1-3).

Grape Harvest

The reaping of a great harvest of grapes from the earth in Rev. 14:17-20 symbolized judgment overtaking the wicked.

The Tree of Life

The fruit-bearing tree of life with healing in its leaves is imagery of God's lifting the curse from the world and blessing all nations by means of the Gospel (Rev.22:2-5).

TRANSFER THEOLOGY

The idea of "common," that is, acquired contamination, is a two-way street that expresses quite well the meaning of "transfer theology."

In the "scapegoat" sacrifice prescribed in Leviticus 16, Aaron was to "lay both his hands on the head of the live goat, and confess over him all the sins of the sons of Israel, and all their transgressions in all their sins, putting them on the head of the goat, and shall send away by the hand of a chosen man into the wilderness. And the goat shall bear on him all their sins to a land in which no one lives. And he shall let the goat go into the wilderness" (Lev.16:21-22).

The laying of hands on the Scapegoat signified the transfer (by pressure) of the people's sins to the animal through their priestly representative. Those sins were then carried far away from them by the goat as he wandered into "no man's land." Yes, God takes away His covenant people's sins...as far away as the east is from the west. The LORD is truly merciful.

On the other hand, "whatever touches the altar shall be clean," according to Exodus 29:37.

These samples of Old Testament transfer theology typified that great spiritual principle of "imputation," a legal concept. Adam's sin was imputed (transferred legally) to all his posterity (Ro.5:12,19). And, Christ's righteousness is imputed to all of God's elect (II Cor.5:21).

Transfer theology is a great blessing, taking salvation out of the hands of spiritually dead men, and resting it in the hands of the omnipotent, sovereign triune God of the Bible. None can snatch believers out of his hand, it being an irrevocable transfer of sin to the Savior, and righteousness to the sheep of his pasture (Jn. 10:28).

This biblical truth stands in strong opposition to humanistic "decisional regeneration" wherein man is purported to exercise his will to choose Jesus apart from God's electing grace and the regenerating work of His Spirit (Titus 3:5,6; Phil 2:13).

PRAISE THE LORD FOR TRANSFER THEOLOGY!

JOHN CALVIN and the DIETARY LAWS

In his commentary on the book of Leviticus, John Calvin concludes that "the prohibition of meats must be counted among the ceremonies which were exercises in the worship of God," even though he admits that "the animals which do not ruminate feed for the most part on filth and excrement."

He criticizes those who allegorize the Scriptures because they elicit mystical senses from its letter in "all sorts of imaginations." But he does endorse the more simple notion, as he puts it, in discussing those animals which parteth the hoof, that, "they who only have a taste for the carnal sense, do not divide the hoof; for, as Paul says, only 'he that is spiritual discerneth all things.' The chewing of the cud ought to follow, duly to prepare and digest the spiritual food; for many gulp down Scripture without profit, because they neither sincerely desire to profit by it, nor seek to refresh their souls by it, as their nourishment; but satisfied with empty delights of knowledge, make no efforts to conform their life to it." He calls it probable analogy to transfer to men what is said about animals and has no definite thought on why God chose some animals to be designated "unclean" except that they, for the most part, feed on excrement.

Commenting on Leviticus 11:4, he says "that an animal, although it may ruminate, shall not be clean unless it cleaves the hoof; and, on the other hand, that the cloven hoof will not be sufficient unless combined with rumination. In these words Moses taught that partial and imperfect purity must not be obtruded upon God. If any choose to think that rumination is the symbol of internal purity, and the cloven hoof of external, his opinion will be a probable one. Since this distinction has occurred to my mind, although I have no taste {no pun intended, I am sure) for subtle speculations, I have thought it well to mention it, yet leaving it free for anyone to accept it or not."

It is very disappointing to see the great teacher of the Protestant Reformation indulge in this sort of allegorizing. One wishes he had offered no comment at all rather than continue to propagate, at least on this topic, the false method of interpretation that ran rampant through the middle ages from about 600 to 1200 A.D., which the Reformation is credited with correcting.

Augustine (354-430 A.D.) started the four-fold method of interpretation; historical, figurative, allegorical, and mystical. The four legs of a table, for instance, stood for the four meanings of the Bible.

For the allegorist, words are just a shell for other than their normal meaning. Nothing really means what it says, or else it has a secret secondary meaning that needs to be mined out of the grammar. The allegorist expects to find a hidden spiritual message within each word of the Bible, and the greater the imagination, the better.

THIRD WORLD CONDITIONS FOSTER TAPEWORM CYSTS

(From the Mail Tribune of Medford, Oregon-Autumn, 1996)

Sue McConnell, an informed specialist with the Centers for Disease Control in Atlanta, says cysticercosis is "a whole lot more common than you would ever think - I get calls every day."

No good statistics are available, however, because the disease is not reportable in the United States. Dr. Allan Campbell, of the Phoenix-based Clinica del Valle community health clinic, says he is now seeing about two cases a year.

Although the common path of infection is consumption of raw or undercooked pork leading to a tapeworm infestation in the gut, followed by self-infection leading to cysts throughout the body, there are other paths.

"Tapeworms are sticky," says McConnell. "It's possible they could spread by food handlers."

One standard medical text, Tropical and Geographical Medicine, (Warren and Mahmoud, McGraw-Hill, 1984) says prevention of human cysticercosis in chronically infected areas is difficult "despite scrupulous personal hygiene and eating habits. The tapeworm eggs, which cause cysticercosis, may be spread by feces, food, water, and perhaps even the air."

In poor countries where people and pigs live in close proximity, infection rates are high. Warren and Mahmoud report that in the slums of northern India more than 10 percent of humans may be infected - and 8 to 10 percent of pigs. In Mexico, perhaps 1 percent of the population may be infected, and the disease likely accounts for 28 percent of all neurological disease. In parts of Africa, cysticercosis may account for 15 percent of all epilepsy cases.

To prevent cross-infection within a family, McConnell says the CDC usually recommends the whole family be checked at once.

Blood tests and CAT scans can help confirm a diagnosis. Unfortunately, Third World immigrants carrying the disease likely can't afford CAT scans. Polly Williams, director of the Clinica del Valle, says her clinic has limited funds for scans, which may cost anywhere from several hundred to over a thousand dollars. Of the clinic's 1,000 clients each month, perhaps 750 have no medical coverage at all.

"That's the difficult thing about what our physicians do," Williams says. "People that come in more than likely are not insured, and sometimes we can't give them the treatment we'd like."

WILL THE REAL BIBLE PLEASE STAND UP ?

The Christian Bible, in the King James Version, is still a best seller, but in modern times a host of new translations have entered into the competition. These are all in updated English and claim to have a greater claim on being the TRUE Word of God because they are alleged to be based upon the oldest and best manuscripts of the New Testament available. This claim is certainly unsubstantiated. In fact, the newer versions, based on a comparative handful of Greek texts, are open to serious challenge, as we shall see.

But first, a word about the Word. Christian thinking is not, and can not be, neutral. It rests upon the presupposition that God exists, "In the beginning God..."(Gen.1:1), and that He reveals Himself to man in the natural order (Psalm 19:1ff; Rom. 1:18ff) and in the Bible, "Thus saith the Lord," being a very common claim of the Scriptures. It is further held, that every jot-and-tittle of the Bible was inspired by God and has, in His good providence, been preserved and handed down to us through the ages (II Peter 1:21; II Tim. 3:16).

Exactly how the preservation of those sixty-six books written by at least forty authors over a sixteen-hundred year period, has occurred, is suitably addressed under the respective headings of the Old and the New Testament Scriptures.

The thirty-nine books of the Hebrew Scriptures were repeatedly, and meticulously, copied and preserved by the Old Covenant Priests, who also instructed the people of God in them for over fifteen hundred years (Deut. 31:11,12,24-26). Because Jesus Christ, the promised Messiah of those Scriptures, quoted them frequently in His earthly ministry, we know that they had been reliably preserved until His time (John 10:35; Mt. 22:29; 4:4,7,10).

The twenty-seven books of the New Testament Greek text were written by Christ's inspired followers (chiefly, the Apostles) after Christ had offered Himself as the perfect, sinless sacrifice for the sins of His elect people, and had arisen from the grave, and ascended to Heaven. He had promised to send the Holy Spirit, second person of the trinity, to give the New Testament writers perfect recall of the events they had witnessed (John 14:25-26). The transmission of those writings down through the centuries was committed to a NEW priesthood, the New Covenant priesthood, which is all believers (I Pet.2:9).

This post-advent transmission was accomplished in the same way that it was under the Old Covenant regime, where the priests copied and recopied the Scriptures. As the years passed, and the churches grew and prospered, sweeping to the north of Jerusalem through Asia minor and then into Europe, the Christians copied and recopied the writings of the inspired writers to meet the growing demand. During the Apostolic era, Christians were keenly aware of the genuineness of the writings, having heard the Apostles preach in person, and then having received letters (epistles) from them. The manuscripts multiplied, and as they started to wear out from constant use, new copies were made. This process went on through the centuries, guided by the Providential hand of God, who is sovereign over the most minute actions of His creatures. And so, it was no problem for God to first inspire writers, and then guide the preservation of those manuscripts from generation to generation long after the original manuscripts had worn out. Trustworthy copies were made and trustworthy copies read and recopied, over and over again, while untrustworthy copies were recognized as such and put aside for the most part. But, you ask, do not uninspired men sometimes make mistakes along this route? Of course, they do. And this is where Godly men, in the exercise of textual criticism, perform their part in the whole divinely moved process.

There are over five thousand ancient manuscripts of the New Testament Scriptures in existence, copies made by the churches as they spread through Asia Minor and into Europe. Many are only fragments, others are entire books, but they are so many that the textual critic can compare them, verse by verse, through the entire New Testament. He may find hundreds of texts in agreement one with the other, and a few that disagree. The obvious conclusion is that those texts in agreement are the trustworthy copies, and the others are then discarded.

Now comes a fly into the ointment. Despite this overwhelming conformity of ancient Scriptures gathered from the part of the world in which the early churches flourished, there are some offbeat manuscripts that differ; off the beaten path of the church's growth, and also off the beaten path of consistent theology. These are chiefly the Alexandrian texts, so called because they were found in Egypt where there is scanty evidence of churches having been established and where heresies existed by the grave-full. Why do modern critics love these few scraps of untrustworthy manuscripts? Because they are the OLDEST manuscripts, having been copied closer to the time that the originals were authored. There are a number of things wrong with this reasoning.

1. Because of the dry climate, manuscripts do not deteriorate very rapidly, so it is only natural that older manuscripts will be found in such a place.

2. Because the manuscripts were not used much, perhaps highly suspect of being untrustworthy copies, they didn't receive much wear, and therefore survived longer.

3. In fact, during the second century the church fathers complained bitterly in their writings of the deliberate alterations made in texts by heretics. It was not a time of no-contest.

4. Some of those manuscripts give evidence that the copier did NOT KNOW GREEK, and precision cannot be accomplished by a mere copy-cat who does not even know the language.

5. One manuscript, named p66 (scholars have a code-numbering system to keep track of the various manuscripts), is probably the oldest (200 A.D.), but it has an average of roughly two mistakes per verse. Age doesn't necessarily mean reliable.

6. Two other Alexandrian manuscripts differ with each other well over 3,000 times; Parchment codices B (Vaticanus) and Aleph (Sinaiticus), both assigned to the fourth century.

7. The strongest argument of all against the Alexandrian texts is that some of them make the Bible contradict itself or teach an outright heresy. For instance:

   a. Jesus is made to be a sinner in Matthew 5:22, which leaves out a clause: "But I tell you that anyone who is angry with his brother will be subject to judgment." Jesus, of course, was on occasion ANGRY with ungodly opponents (Mark 3:5). It's no wonder unbelieving liberals love the NIV, for it makes Jesus equal to the rest of humanity. The majority Greek text (Textus Receptus/ King James) correctly quotes Jesus as saying, "But I say unto you that each of you who is angry with his brother WITHOUT A CAUSE shall be liable to the judgment"(emphasis added). Anger for a righteous reason is not a sin. Jesus was not a sinner! Ask your Pastor why he and the school he matriculated from promote the use of the NIV non-Bible.

b. The Alexandrian text used in the NIV makes Jesus just another man, descending from a human father, not the sinless son of the virgin Mary who conceived by the Holy Spirit. Alexandrian texts Aleph, B, and W say: "The [child's] FATHER and mother marveled at what was said about him [Jesus]" (Luke 2:33). But the majority of Greek texts read: "And Joseph was marveling, also his mother, at the things being said concerning him."

c.) Col. 1:14, according to the Alexandrian cultists behind the NIV (and other bastard translations), omits the BLOOD-bought redemption secured by Christ for His elect, when it says: "In whom we have redemption, the forgiveness of sins," while in the 20th verse they keep the blood. The majority text is consistent: "In whom we have redemption through his blood, the forgiveness of sins." Humanists of all shades love a Jesus who didn't shed his blood for sinners, and they love any contradiction or supposed problem in a passage of Scripture since they don't believe it is the inspired Word of God.

This small sampling of how ancient heretics have wrought havoc with the Scriptures through the scheming of unbelieving modern scholars, such as Westcott and Hort, the fathers of modern textual criticism, and through the acceptance of their views by modern "scholars" and their dupes in seminaries and churches, should serve to alarm you and move you to explore this issue in greater depth. W & H, by the way, also have a unique method of translating the Bible, called DYNAMIC EQUIVALENCE. By this they discard the doctrine of the verbal inspiration of the Scriptures in favor of using words they deem more "dynamic"...that is, "but it seems to read better to me if we say it our way!" Some verses in their "translations" fail to translate most of the words that are IN the text, while supplying many words that CANNOT be found in the text. This method has nothing but contempt for the jot-and-tittle inspiration and reliability of the Scriptures of both the Old and the New Testaments.

Hence, it is not difficult to see why a phrase like, "in saying this, Jesus declared all foods clean," has found its way into the text of modern versions of Mark 7:14-23. Theological swine, like their beastly counterparts, like to rush in and rend the truth of Scripture.

Many faithful men have been raised up by God to expose this farce that parades as a scientific method. They say, "No, we cannot trust unbelieving textual critics to dictate which manuscripts we are to regard as the Word of God!" It is NOT a NEUTRAL science. Every thought discipline has its presupposition(s). The Christian approach to textual criticism has those presuppositions noted at the beginning of this article. God exists, and He has revealed Himself to mankind through the Scriptures of the Old and New Testaments. These Scriptures are consistent and uniform in doctrine. We reject "dynamic equivalence" as a blasphemous and satanically inspired practice that raises man's wisdom and understanding above God's.

Below are listed a few books, some out of print, others reprinted, and some fairly new, all of which deal with this very important subject.

Books by John W. Burgon (British Scholar of the last century)

THE WOMAN TAKEN IN ADULTERY
THE LAST TWELVE VERSES OF MARK

Books by Edward F Hills

BELIEVING BIBLE STUDY, KEY TO THE SPACE AGE (1967)
THE KING JAMES VERSION DEFENDED (1956)

THE CORRUPTION OF THE WORD
by Kevin James (1990)

Books by Jay Green, Sr.

UNHOLY HANDS ON THE BIBLE, AN INTRODUCTION TO TEXTUAL CRITICISM
    Volume I (1990) Contains Burgon reprints
    Volume II (1992) Examines modern texts

THE REVISION REVISED, Centennial Edition
[1883-1983]-May, 1991
    Three articles by John W. Burgon, B.D.
    I. THE NEW GREEK TEXT
    II. THE NEW ENGLISH VERSION
    III. WESTCOTT AND HORT'S NEW TEXTUAL THEORY

THE GNOSTICS, THE NEW VERSIONS, AND
THE DEITY OF CHRIST (1994)

Mr. Green, who has devoted his life to this study, has also published THE HOLY BIBLE, THE MODERN KING JAMES VERSION as well as an Interlinear Old and New Testament.

Mr. Green operates through the Sovereign Grace Trust Fund and publishes a book review & discount sales catalog, NEWS AND VIEWS OF THE CHRISTIAN LITERATURE WORLD, INC., 705B South Earl Ave., P.O. Box 4998, Lafayette, Ind. 47903 (800) 447-9142

This is not a complete listing of such works, but through Mr. Green's publications alone one may become well informed on this subject.

Order Form

QTY	TITLE	AMOUNT
	The Catechism For Young Children;	
___	Book I; Q1 thru Q71 .... $1.75 ea.	_____
___	Book II; Q72 thru Q145 .... 1.75 ea.	_____
	How Shall We Worship God?	
___	Family Catechism; 39Q .... 1.75 ea.	_____
___	Bible Books Memory Chart (3+ 1.50 ea.) .... 2.00 ea.	_____
___	The Biblical Dietary Laws 9.00	_____
___	Biblical Economics In Comics 9.00	_____
___	Essay on Money 4.00	_____
___	God's Law for Modern Man 6.00	_____
___	In These Last Days 6.00	_____
___	Money, Banking and Usury 4.00	_____
___	Reading & Understanding the Bible 6.00	_____
___	Revelation, the Book of 6.00	_____
___	The Forgotten Minority (Psalmody) 3.00	_____
___	Super Bug... Gospel in the Woods 3.00	_____
___	Water, Water Everywhere *(Flood)* 4.00	_____
	Westminster Confession of Faith	
___	*(1 sheet outline with cartoons)* .... 100 for 6.00	_____
___	Westminster Shorter Catechism with Cartoons ... 19.95	_____
___	Who Stopped the Clock? *(Daniel 9)* 3.00	_____
___	The Worship Principle 3.00	_____

Postage and Handling Rates　　**Sub-total** .... $ _____
Orders up to $20 – $2.00　　　　　**Postage** .... $ _____
Over $20 – 10% / Foreign – 20%　**Amount Enclosed** $ _____

Name _____
Street _____
City _____ State _____ Zip _____

Order From:
VIC LOCKMAN – P.O. Box 1396, Yreka, CA 96097

Order Form

QTY	TITLE	AMOUNT
___	The Catechism For Young Children; Book I; Q1 thru Q71 .... $1.75 ea.	_____
___	Book II; Q72 thru Q145 .... 1.75 ea.	_____
___	How Shall We Worship God? Family Catechism; 39Q .... 1.75 ea.	_____
___	Bible Books Memory Chart (3+ 1.50 ea.) .... 2.00 ea.	_____
___	The Biblical Dietary Laws 9.00	_____
___	Biblical Economics in Comics 9.00	_____
___	Essay on Money 4.00	_____
___	God's Law for Modern Man 6.00	_____
___	In These Last Days 6.00	_____
___	Money, Banking and Usury 4.00	_____
___	Reading & Understanding the Bible 6.00	_____
___	Revelation, the Book of 6.00	_____
___	The Forgotten Minority (Psalmody) 3.00	_____
___	Super Bug... Gospel in the Woods 3.00	_____
___	Water, Water Everywhere *(Flood)* 4.00	_____
___	Westminster Confession of Faith *(1 sheet outline with cartoons)* .... 100 for 6.00	_____
___	Westminster Shorter Catechism with Cartoons ... 19.95	_____
___	Who Stopped the Clock? *(Daniel 9)* 3.00	_____
___	The Worship Principle 3.00	_____

Postage and Handling Rates
Orders up to $20 – $2.00
Over $20 – 10% / Foreign – 20%

Sub-total .... $ _____
Postage .... $ _____
Amount Enclosed $ _____

Name _____
Street _____
City _____ State _____ Zip _____

**Order From:
VIC LOCKMAN – P.O. Box 1396, Yreka, CA 96097**

Order Form

QTY	TITLE	AMOUNT
	The Catechism For Young Children;	
___	Book I; Q1 thru Q71 .... $1.75 ea.	_____
___	Book II; Q72 thru Q145 .... 1.75 ea.	_____
	How Shall We Worship God?	
___	Family Catechism; 39Q .... 1.75 ea.	_____
___	Bible Books Memory Chart (3+ 1.50 ea.) .... 2.00 ea.	_____
___	The Biblical Dietary Laws 9.00	_____
___	Biblical Economics In Comics 9.00	_____
___	Essay on Money 4.00	_____
___	God's Law for Modern Man 6.00	_____
___	In These Last Days 6.00	_____
___	Money, Banking and Usury 4.00	_____
___	Reading & Understanding the Bible 6.00	_____
___	Revelation, the Book of 6.00	_____
___	The Forgotten Minority (Psalmody) 3.00	_____
___	Super Bug... Gospel in the Woods 3.00	_____
___	Water, Water Everywhere *(Flood)* 4.00	_____
	Westminster Confession of Faith	
___	*(1 sheet outline with cartoons)* .... 100 for 6.00	_____
___	Westminster Shorter Catechism with Cartoons ... 19.95	_____
___	Who Stopped the Clock? *(Daniel 9)* 3.00	_____
___	The Worship Principle 3.00	_____

Postage and Handling Rates   **Sub-total** .... $ _____
Orders up to $20 – $2.00   **Postage** .... $ _____
Over $20 – 10% / Foreign – 20%   **Amount Enclosed** $ _____

Name_____
Street_____
City _____ State _____ Zip _____

Order From:
VIC LOCKMAN – P.O. Box 1396, Yreka, CA 96097

Order Form

QTY	TITLE	AMOUNT
	The Catechism For Young Children;	
___	Book I; Q1 thru Q71 .... $1.75 ea.	_____
___	Book II; Q72 thru Q145 .... 1.75 ea.	_____
	How Shall We Worship God?	
___	Family Catechism; 39Q .... 1.75 ea.	_____
___	Bible Books Memory Chart (3+ 1.50 ea.) .... 2.00 ea.	_____
___	The Biblical Dietary Laws 9.00	_____
___	Biblical Economics in Comics 9.00	_____
___	Essay on Money 4.00	_____
___	God's Law for Modern Man 6.00	_____
___	In These Last Days 6.00	_____
___	Money, Banking and Usury 4.00	_____
___	Reading & Understanding the Bible 6.00	_____
___	Revelation, the Book of 6.00	_____
___	The Forgotten Minority (Psalmody) 3.00	_____
___	Super Bug... Gospel in the Woods 3.00	_____
___	Water, Water Everywhere *(Flood)* 4.00	_____
	Westminster Confession of Faith	
___	*(1 sheet outline with cartoons)* .... 100 for 6.00	_____
___	Westminster Shorter Catechism with Cartoons... 19.95	_____
___	Who Stopped the Clock? *(Daniel 9)* 3.00	_____
___	The Worship Principle 3.00	_____

Postage and Handling Rates
Orders up to $20 – $2.00
Over $20 – 10% / Foreign – 20%

Sub-total .... $ _____
Postage .... $ _____
Amount Enclosed $ _____

Name _____
Street _____
City _____ State _____ Zip _____

Order From:
VIC LOCKMAN – P.O. Box 1396, Yreka, CA 96097